C000185495

BREAKING ... & OTHER POEMS

ALISON BRACKENBURY
Breaking Ground
and other poems

CARCANET

Acknowledgements are due to the editors of *Times Literary Supplement, Poetry Review, PN Review, Poetry Wales, Listener, New Statesman, Poetry Now* (B.B.C. 3), *Some Contemporary Poets of Britain and Ireland* (Carcanet), *Stand* and *Outposts*, where some of these poems first appeared.

First published in 1984 by
CARCANET PRESS LIMITED
208–212 Corn Exchange Buildings
Manchester M4 3BQ

All rights reserved.

Copyright © Alison Brackenbury 1984

British Library Cataloguing in Publication Data
Brackenbury, Alison
Breaking ground and other poems
I. Title
821'.914   PR6052.R236

ISBN 0-85635-503-8

The publisher acknowledges financial assistance from
the Arts Council of Great Britain

Typeset in England by Paragon Photoset, Aylesbury
Printed in England by SRP Ltd, Exeter

Contents

I
Assorted Poems

The birds

I come back to the students' shabby cloakroom,
To listen to the birds. Their nest is out of sight;
Leaning from windows, in the cool, comes near
Their high dusk crying. Sparrows? no, too sweet.
Starlings? I would not think so. Swallows, yes.
I watch the brown hill shrink. I hear
Sea in their voices, continents of heat.

Rented rooms

Night stole away my reason to be there —
that routine note which missed the post. I came
out of the throaty mist, the New Year's air,
stared, at the dim house which showed no name,
called to a girl, who rattled past her bike,
blowing her fog-damp scarf, winter's hot cheeks.

The first door I pushed open from their hall
gaped a conservatory, shadowed: full
of spoiled ferns once, sweet geraniums.
Now it held bikes, askew. It breathed back all
the cold of first streets, lingering on stairs —
the outside door blows open — no one cares
to clean: from Christmas, ivy curls in sprays,
dark, in rolls of dirt. Who went away
leaving this television blank above
a rolled-up quilt? Quick: drop the printed note
on the hall's floor.

                    It echoes back again
the deep sea chill of fog, the waves of dust,
my wonder at a room's dimmed lights. .
Need, then:
the stairs to silence; not to own, but love.

Pantomime

Cinderella, Cinderella
here in Swindon waiting room
the buffet blind has closed its silver eye.
The light is harsh and yellow
the stars glint white as chilblain
and midnight yawns too close.
                              Yet he asks: 'why
does a young girl, like yourself, not go to dances?
real, ball-room dances? I meself
would be at one next week: but I'm on nights.'
He is ageing, kind and Irish: the finest drunken flush
glows child-pink, where his red hair lies thin.
His feet tap to his whistling. Out of his coat flash bright
tins — 'I won a raffle —' peaches, cream;
'which always come in handy? Eh?' The Prince, unkempt as Buttons
ruffles in the ashes, coughing, dancing. He has seen
a train: 'it must be yours — ' I smile.
                              I hear the lost mice squeak.

O he's still there, I'm sure of it: all winter's killing weeks,
though I have caught the dusty train and gone
with the pale-cheeked foreign lady; whom he so annoyed
she hid behind her fur and tried to sleep:
He is still there: wild-whistling, pigeon-toed
spinning down, by each girl in the room,
lit like a rose against the outer cold
he sees each train glide out except his own,
he waits: till heartless night shall dance to gold

        and puts off, yes, for ever, going home.

Whose window?

Whose window are you gazing through,
Whose face is stilled between your hands?
The glass glows deeper than your eyes
Where quick lights sink: as feet through sands.

Into your darkness first snow drives,
No soft meander, aimless drift,
But straight as water. Crumbling bright,
Sharp crystals flash, as if they lived.

Now when the great wind throbs the door
When street-light and small hedge are drowned
My face turns open into night.
I am not safe. No, I am found
Melting the hard bolts back. The hall
Is filled with dark air, ice-clouds blow:

A warm face sleeps. I am the snow,
Uncatch your window. Let me through.

February, March, April

February

Now, all the mist has sunk and left
great drops on rose briars,
a scuffle of ice in the water butt,
the snowdrops, yesterday dull with ice
now slender, white, and bare:

Now sky drifts far above our roofs
the street sings; churches, radios;
drills; your rough brush sweeping
paths to the washed shore:

the wind blows sea-blue, hints to me
lost heat, its summer's distance,
this house breathes soft, the air lies kind

      'Now you are reconciled.'
      Shall I believe— what I only see
      in mist— the promised world?

March

The clocks are changed. The houses die away
To land: the bicycle whirrs in the lane.
The precious hour holds off the last smoulder
Of day: the hazing fields, and my bare arms
Rise warm with light.

Rose, quick blue, the late clouds trail and fly;
From flooding sky-filled ponds ducks call again
Soft on the brim of sleep. The grass fields have been rolled
In swathes of green, dull silver; soon the farms
Will turn out stock to sleep through open night

Deepening the dark with breath, and in the day
The ponies, the tall hunter too, will roll;
And lie a moment, slumped into the ground
Against the heat and grass scent; feel perhaps
Long as the shadow, quicker than the sun.

But now, through summer's first day the ground soaks
Slow light, in spring's cold water, it unlocks
Bruised grass from ground, and us, sprung back from dark
By chance, and colder clicking of our clocks.

April

A card from Venice. Sitting on the stairs,
Hearing the rain mutter in the trees,
Desire rises green as the bronze horses
Step soft to silence in the high salt air.

I cannot see it steady; filmed at night
Dark alleys dip with water, frightened faces.
In pictures its most solid streets and places
Are burnt in air, dissolved in light.

In heat of sleep, as water glimmers hands,
It washes me, in thoughts of you.
I saw it once in darkness, from a plane
Lights thrown against black sea:
                              the place
Which is not, which we journey to.

Warm rain, green spikes of chestnut flowers unlit,
the changing ground slips sudden from my feet.
The waters of the sharp buds quiver, break.
The cities sink. Summer is what we make.

Breaking

Something has happened,
Something in raw dark
gone between us. Now
the bicycle slips
spinning on air
without power —
chains are easy to fix —

but I,
crouched, for half an hour
in the streetlight's cold eye
drop the broken hedge-sticks,
leave the links meshed hopelessly

begin to walk
through the waves of flu
day held at bay,
to shiver. Click
of the wheel changes,
dragging cracks
of pavements, the children's
the old woman's way
I never tread. Rain flicks. I see

Blossom — Drained by the streetlight, pale
it rests on air, a tree whose name
I never learned; half winter's, frail
rain-licked, it gleams.
Now only calm
washes me, a car-lit rain.
The branch is dipped behind my sight
with one, marching, man I meet:
whose spaniel strains the lead: who does not speak.

Once I would have been quite sure
walking to you:
that you, head filled with accidents

would come to find me. 'No.'
I say: as truly 'it is dark'; as perfect tiredness
touched, with petal, weighed with wind
will not resent, feels no distress

but breaks, high flower filled with wind
into a thousand things —
when round the last road's corner swings
the slow car, dull blue as night's sky
when you stare palely at me, I
running to you, though the rain's blurred glass
will let no sound through, speak your name —
Nothing can happen,
be the same.

Last week

Last week I had two rows with my superior,
my best friend chose to leave. There was a bomb scare:
we shivered for an hour, among clouds of smoke and daisies
(the smoke was cigarettes, they found no bomb).
I promised next, to strike, risking the dull future —
not the best of weeks, in short. Again the lilac
hangs heavy over other people's fences
and when no one is looking, after rain
I draw the sprays close to me, breathing slower
brush from my face the cold and vivid water.
The martins have returned, from unimagined seas'
wind-blinded miles, as sudden as they left
their bow of wings, stubbed tails, boldly black
wheel and turn above the crumbling flats;
how tall they make the houses look. The sky
stays further than I thought, further and higher.

Half-day

Padding the green alleys of my grass
Watching jackdaws crest upon the roof
I sit, red dock seed rustling by my head.
Great hollyhocks sway up from last year's roots.

My neighbour's child cries, her mother shouts
'I'm busy with the ironing! You must come in or out!'

So she goes in. And it is sad, the quiet,
The grass still warm, seed-silver. Will she lift
Her face from cloth's slow steam: will she find out
Ironing is duty; summer is a gift?

The dealer's dog

'Good dog', I called. But still she barked.
No dog has ever bitten me.
The dealer's dogs mark rights of way
By rushing through the nettles, rusty
Harrows, bales of mouldered hay
The horse sniffs softly; jumping at me.
She was a hound: dull yellow, white,
She sprang as I leaned to the gate,
Her teeth nipped through my padded boot.
Did she guard puppies? Heavy teats
Swung as she bayed, rushed the closed gate.

'The children down Caernarvon Road
Caught a chicken last night, poured
Petrol on; set it alight.
Would you like that lot down your road?'

What has been done here? God or Devil,
He calls to her. Her eyes grow hard,
Yellow, stilled. She beats her tail,
She wriggles down the concrete yard.

Recorders

London is full of them, the people walking
With wires in their pockets, wires on sun-red skin
Throbbed from the recorder to the receiving ear.
You can pick them out at once: islanded in traffic,
Their faces pleased and blind: most private people.

Sad — I thought once — how they are shut away,
Alone, with sound. But now I wonder,
Leant in the cool hollow of the plane tree
Scanning St. James' Park, where grey-haired men
Spread papers' sheets to crouch beneath the sun;
Where secretaries wriggle their white toes
Into the kind, worn grass. Now if you took
The deadening phones away, what would you hear —
Black waves of noise as starlings darken evening;
Or what a bird calls, in the spreading leaves,
Our most unlikely music?

Apple country

I am living, quite unplanned, by apple country.
Worcesters come the earliest: sea-green
With darkest red, even the flesh, veined pink.
They have a bloom no hand can brush away
sweet breath made visible. But do not think
to have them through the dark days: they'll not keep,
For that choose Coxes flecked with gold
Which wrinkle into kindness, winter's fires.

Where I was born they let no flowering trees
in the bare fields, which grow my dreams, which hold
only the lasting crops: potato, wheat.
How low the houses crouch upon their soil
with fruitless hedges; at the barn's end, cars:

none yours. I have no art for probing back
to such dark roots. Yet if you pass this place
Though skies shine lean with frost, no softness dapples
White wall to cave of leaf, yet stranger, knock.

For I will give you apples.

Invitations

Come outside, to the season
of prodigal richness,
apples rolled in gutters
stained and gently red.
Gleaming, too careless,

hear again, the sound run under voices —
not the voice of madness, but the dew
parting the rough air like stems of grass.
I have heard there too

the women, talking at the small dark gates.
'She lived in Tewkesbury, beside the river.'
I hear no ending through that rush,
the voices murmur,

its sadness; its slow promise. I have never
turned so resolutely to the body
dark from the Turkish sun, and lit by you
so people watch me, puzzled, and I cannot
explain, the warmth ebbs through

leaving the fingertips. And will it ever
return? as I have heard
upon a column, in a foreign city
rose an angel, burdened down with gold;
as all this air. The craneflies whirred

through misted grass. The angel too is gone,
built, to mark a peace. Now lingering
upon the empty step I stand, still listening
through all the shadows of our night: to wings.

Inside

Prisoners of the top floor
those who hurt children,
who laid bombs in Ireland, all
unsafe in prison,
while others sit, three to a cell, yawn
together at benches
these are kept in:

they poke their food out on to sills:
and when great gulls heave down, and beat
clouded grey wings, folded from sky,
they close wire nooses round their feet.

The boy: a trusty: and the guard
race out across the wire-edged yard
where the bird falls and flings.

The young man, who works in the stores
Has real coffee; by grey doors
Sniffs; smiles. He sees no wings.

Moving

There is a place where you would always live —
a village; a grey house; a quiet coast
glimpsed for a moment when you were in love,
brimming to the window of a coach
or scarcely seen at all but in all maps
pulsing like a vein into the heart.

The place I saw was Hastings. But in rain
the endless sea is blind.
Where are the tender lights which we saw strung
from the high room we rented, the long slide
men washed down every day? I twist my head,
see rain-green walls. 'For Sale.' So she is dead

Her great jugs ringed with roses; whose man died
oh, years before; what was she, eighty? when
she dragged a new case to us on her stairs,
'for my great-niece; another fits inside.'
That was when she showed us the stripped wall
barred, with dark ships' timbers, bulging bare;
on seas of autumn night I heard them creak —
turned house, turned ship — trying to move elsewhere.

Under trees

The garden is withdrawing, the wind is raw
For rain. The grass is now too wet to sit
Although the cat lies still, where hay stalks bend
Unharvested, the spiders hunch and float.
I found the first walnut. The green husk tore
In ragged petals, and the damp shell wore
Black in my fingers' grain. Shadowed, I stand
In my new full-sleeved blouse, my fingers swollen
And feel, through mine, the shape of other hands,

Younger — or older? For I always loved
The very old: who easily turn young
Have shed all pride; who can remember
Horse-chestnuts, cold from morning, with the clinging
Pink thumbprint of the shell; who would have rubbed
Those continents of dark and blood,
Those tiny worlds. Yet I have known
Others; neither young nor old; face dappled
By walnuts' wide split leaves which wind has torn.

I think first, of a room above a city.
To keep a view is costly, to watch trees
Stirred and open from above — that wind outside
Too suddenly is autumn's. The room sees
Far; its still air dries, is warm and easy
But for the taste of ashes in the throat.
No, how should I blame you? We would hide;
And yet, most people rise to aching light.
The walnut stains my hand; brown barbed seeds cling.
Brushing my cuff's rich purple, I begin
Still beneath the blind wind, to take sides

To choose some worlds, withdraw from others, as
The sap slides in the stalk, as the cat sleeps
Under the fitful wind. There is no time
To do all things. Have you, at last
Realised this? I wonder. Would you laugh

To hear that I have, wilfully, sprung sideways
Out of my moneyed job, all at a time
When no one pays for work, so I may have
A child? Have I then, at last, come down?

Inside the dry bank spreads a cyclamen
Which I have planted and which I forget
Until each autumn, under deeper dews
It sends up one leaf only, pinched and wet.
Though I have others which have thrived, now spring
In white and scentless flurries, poised, and flying,
Yet I have bent to this. For as I trust
As you said, soft, its making must take years,
A garden will return; and without us.

Trees

We are past the Christmas trees, in their wide windows
hung with light, like fruit. They shine all day.
We have watched the fields, where the moon is rising:
smudged, solemn mouth. Above us, white stars grow:
huge and bare, spread over earth:
a tree of light, a tree of snow.

Climbing

There was a snow line
on the hill path
where white crumbled into folds
of willow bark, the spread
green glow of ivy.

Turn back now —

So we went on.
For all the springing water
is alive, swirls foam
of sap or the land's poison,
till snow dusts every stone

whirls black and brings the sky down:
Tiny walkers shrink
though we found their slow bootmarks.
Our opened eyes must blink

our feet slip on the good road —
Turn. It's time
to back away from winter,
the white-hung wire; climb
back to the wet green valley
exhausted, sleep.
                    I hold
no measure of new snow lines
high country of the cold.

Messenger

Ice in his mane
Across the empty land
Past crows, the buzzing poles
He is coming

down the tall, the wide streets
the old and narrow
he is treading
always the same pace,
his head lowered
into the wind's glare.

A few handfuls of corn
Will keep him walking.
Would you and I survive?
Yet, when he arrives

You will have no stable,
Let him graze a while
in the small garden
where thawing earth turns black.
Be good to him:
Before you send him back.

Decorating

It is simpler than they tell you. Yes, I sit
Trembling with exhaustion; but the tree
Is wedged against the ceiling. If you buy
A sprawling Christmas tree of six feet high
To green a meagre room — yet it will fit:
String looped round window-catches anchors it.

The windows will be closed until the spring.
Ask them, the people who would cut and splinter
Your spreading days: how will they last our winter
In well-lit rooms; warmed through by drink or love?
It is a mass of detail, they will sing,
The needles raining dryly from above.

The crown is supple yet; long red buds cling
Although the root is gone— Not so the trees
Rearing out the park to a bare sky:
The ash, bark wrinkling like a beast's grey skin,
The chestnut, thin twigs rising up in seas.
All the hunger roaring through the wind
Will not be unfamiliar to the trees

Bending beneath it. Be what you have seen —
The shopping list is crumpled and set by.
The tree stands massive by the empty pane
As you bend to the door, fumbling the key.
Where are the bells, the silvered birds or stars?
Gone from us in the opening: in the pause
Which spreads to arms its bare and burning green.

Harvests

The barley is silk, look, purple, silver,
its wild colours. The swallows swim it,
the insects hide from the heavy sky.

Do not rain:
till I have crossed
the unknown streets
and found him there
Till I stroke his thin wrist, his hair,
do not rain.

Let swallows hold the heavy skies,
wheat, its wild colours.

The story continues

The park's a glimmer of black, a haze of rain,
Blown lights mislead us down the open paths
You offer your umbrella. But it is you I want.
In the strange, lit room, again
I cannot touch you; and I watch
Your mouth twitch and your smile slant
In tiredness, till you send me home,
The humming hotel room:

I overwind my watch: which dies.
My yawns check at its quiet
I shake it hard — Is no one near
More skilled: more patient? I have tried
All that I knew; and now I wait
Next day, a final meeting.
Closed in my hands, frail as a bird,
I hold time's heart, still beating.

Monday

The air was dark with rain, the day
Held little promise. And I stared
At all the bills, the things to do:
Then I saw you there

in the high room, yawning, staring
at the dull page, in the lamp's glare.

I laughed. Love is not easy, cannot
will us one or win us time.
Weeks fray us open like a knot.
Worn: all separate: we shine.

Castle

There are lilies in the lake, the lilies of still water
Which part for nodding ducks and close again.
I cannot see my face, they are so close,
Half-opened only, swayed, red stem to stem;
I cross the trembling bridge. Held in the other
Bank, an arch of broken stone pipes gapes
Five silted throats from which no waters fall.
My eye's edge sees — but that would be too strange —
White open mouths of orchids on a wall.

Around the clock is painted a blue heaven
On which the sun's great cycle gilds, and sings.
I cross the yard, bare even of a cat,
Or outstretched dog; or stir of pigeon's wings.
The arches of the yard are white and even
The brass knob of the door is smudged by hands
And I am slower, heavy as the clouds
Which move across the upper sky in pairs,
Now I have reached my certain journey's end
Turning the corner, climbing the closed stairs.

The window is set open and the door
Was never locked. The carpet, once complete
With hunting dogs, tall pairs of gold-chained birds
Is worn down to dark thread, by other feet.
My foot brushes a plate left on the floor
With the dark skins of fruit; fresh apricots
Whose bloom is gone: whose scent would still hang there
If the room were shuttered, closed and not
Open to this sudden cool of air.

I must come here. I must come, many times
Though there is nothing more that I can see
Inside the room or all its passageways
Where small sounds run, too far ahead of me;
No order, day or night, disturbs the chimes.
Yet I may see — if once, I do not watch —

The glint of the stone roof in dark, the moth
Flown before I touch it. I may catch
A hidden breath; the fluttered, warm, black cloth.

Leaving present

I wonder: what happened to those flowers?
Before a neighbour knocked upon your door
Did you get them into water? If not, they would have died.
So the flower-woman said, screwing up her eyes
Against the light; repeating; they love water.

They were scabious, cool blue. When I returned
I saw them nod, flushed purple, on the hill.
Great butterflies broke up from them, new peacocks
Flashing black wings. The horse reached out to them
Stretching, for a mouthful, but I stopped him.

Untouchable flowers.
To buy them, or to let them die
Is not our end. They rustle through the hands.
They are alive. And what I saw
Came for, is true: the cloud-warm hill: and there
A litter of blue petal, upon your tidy floor.

Mending

I twist into my thread
the haze
of your close hair; and bitter gaze

sharp as my strokes. The cotton's strong,
must bear impatient tugs, the long
fret of friction,

Will you care,
when this thread snaps —
to repair?

The wicked godmother

They were quite right, to think I would not do.
I would forget your birthday, would not buy
The customary prayerbook in white leather
Which in its box, remains unused for ever.
I was the one — but that's a little thing —
Who came in with blue hair to see your christening.

It was my voice which whispered to the crumbs
Advice only less strange than breathing is.
Ignore your dolls, wear wild clothes, although
You keep at home, start out upon great journeys.

Leaving

I scarcely notice trains. At our garden's end,
They have become a deepening of the wind
A shudder between voices, or a hum
Rivalling, in my ancient radio
The GI stations and the Russian anthem.
Yawning, in grey air of five o'clock
I kiss you at the station. You are going
To Hungary. I walk the hill streets back

I do not meet a soul. Scarcely awake
I think of the old cleaner's tales. He took
A train for three days, through Australian plains,
A blue unyielding sky, dry for ten years;
Saw clusters of white houses. Hundreds of miles from rain
From any other men — how do they live?
I miss you; but I do not cry. Each garden
Rustles with birds. The slanting wires give

That peculiar shudder; for your train,
Past the road's dip, where I might have seen
The blue and yellow flash — and you, my face.
I gaze through fences, curtained caravans.
I hear the wheels beat, the cutting race
The sound ahead: until the dull air sings
Without people or clear sky: a grey wide place
Shivering and shadowed, under wings.

Sleep. I must sleep again. Against my chin
Fresh from her fights, the young cat finds a berth.
As bottles clink, the new train draws away —
Letters — milk — your pocket's bread — we sway,
Shaken, in our iron veins, to earth.

Medine in Turkey

'Today' said Hassan — through a mouthful of honey —
'A girl will come who speaks French.' There came
A girl with straight brown hair, her eyes
Flecked with gold, a stiller honey.
Her French was pure and soft. Her name
Was Medine. Her paid study
Ended when her father died.
'Maintenant — j'aide ma mère. Je lis.'

'Je lis Freud,' she ventured, bare feet firm
On the rug's blurred leaves. She lived next door.
Each house leads to a tiny yard
With a dusty tree; white chickens squirm
In favourite hollows. She never saw
France; she sat, this grave brown child
Ten years younger than myself, unmarried
Alight, in their cool best room. She smiled.

There is no answer. Scholarships?
France, too, has hot bored villages
With girls who read all afternoon.
The arranged husband, or their child's care
Will not close up that watchful face
Flecked by lace curtains, endless sun;
Unmoved, she listens for the place
Where the book closes, where the footsteps run.

Metamorphosis

You have become — an honorary cat.
Don't laugh; you should be proud. For yours
Are not gold eyes; I have not felt your claws.

Yet I am sure you blink in pools of sunlight
You are fastidious. My cats deplore
My coats and papers scattered on the floor

But curl there: temporarily. They are poised for
The new moon's sudden glitter through the hedge
The better world, down the dark garden's edge,

Will also melt from judgement. Horses are
Good or bad; crash fences; shy at cars.
Cats simply are. And change, as you; who bored
Burn at my room's centre: gold-eyed, clawed.

Supervision

The cats looked up as I fetched keys and said,
'No good will come of this. Look at the rain —
Your feet will be soaked black by it.
Turn up the fire now, stay with us instead.'

The cats stretched paws as I picked up my coat
They blinked, a little sternly. 'It's a way
You haven't driven much. Now think again
Undo those buttons; pour us milk and stay.'

The smallest cat, as I went to the door
Sprang down and followed me: no, not pursuing:
She sat before my feet. Her tawny eyes
Dilated, gold and hard. 'What are you doing?'

It's not my human nature to know that.
I only guess when I return, the bright
Unnecessary light will flood and spoil
A cat's good conversation with the night.

Brooklands

Between the fast road and the private school
A dark and shaggy hedge takes out the view.
Does water rustle in a garden's fold —
Why else the sprawling name, still slanted blue
Beside the locked door? Was it ever sold?
We could not afford it. But the sale
Brought no one here to live. Viburnums, pale
Tight heads of bud which whiten winter, grow
Glossy, unchecked — a hedge now ten feet high
Lets the front door, blind upstairs windows show.

Late in the summer, in surprising heat,
I cycled past through evening, slowly, tired.
Someone had pushed open a high window
An old man sat there writing. As I stared
He raised his eyes: looked calmly back at me.
So they have moved in, at last, I thought.
Next day the long net curtains lay as tight
Across the glass as they had always been;
The door was shut. Was it a neighbour's house
Which I had watched instead? What have I seen?

I do not know. I neither grieve nor care
If someone sorting out their bills, next door,
Had reached and thrust the window up for air,
If it was the surveyor sent at last
To check the rot. The great red dock seeds rust,
The gravel's sunlight, celandines in flower.
The stream runs out of sight. I trust that most
Hearts live haunted. I have seen my ghost.

Heather and Melanie

I was eighteen when I joined that shop,
Selling sunglasses I forgot to dust,
Talked women into liking. Just
Back from an edge: you find your days
Bricks, on a floor. You pick them up
But wince at their joins, tenderly.
Heather stood by the next counter

Straightening the clouding, silky scarves;
Thin as a sparrow, she coughed and talked.
She had quick bright eyes, but her skin was poor.
In some secret care she rubbed it raw
On ankles, round her smudging eyes.

We tread a line: which is not there.
The ground parts slowly. But I picked
Each work day up; at half past ten
Sat eating buns in the dark canteen
When Heather fingered cigarettes.
She had a friend named Melanie
Whom they all knew; who once worked there
While very young; had long fair hair.
'A pretty face.' An older girl
Said Melanie had leukemia.

Heather spent each day off with her
Slept Saturday night in the backstreet pub
Where Melanie lived with a grandmother:
Who, one Sunday, brought up breakfast —
'Bacon!' said Heather, 'we woke up
And smelt it there —' Did Melanie eat?
Where was the street? low upstairs room
Papered with winter roses?

The grandmother rang, when Melanie died,
Heather listened. No; she would stay
Perhaps go early. I looked round,

She had turned to the pillar, shaking,
The scarves still smooth — and through her hands
I saw her face: a bursting red.
As all the blood rushed from her heart
From her thin bones, to help her cry.

They sent her home. Soon Lorraine said —
Lorraine, the plump and clear-skinned girl
Who helped on scarves — that she had left,
She worked in a greengrocer's now.
She liked it; but the door stood propped
So it was cold

Our shop was hot.
They put me on to toys, which broke.
Parents returned them. Personnel
Said think of retail management.

I thought about it. And I think
Of Heather. I have left that town
Which calls itself a city. But,
Who knows? I might go back and want
Cabbage, early apples, go

Into a shop. By glassy grapes
Swollen melons, curling beans
I know her coughing. There she stands
Huddled in sky-blue cardigans,
Weighing potatoes: in frozen hands.

The food department

It is the glutton's dream, the monk's nightmare:
Old Hell might hold such ovens. Under black
Iron plates, the dragons of the gas roar back,
The students — though no angels — smile, stand clear
In white. They chop up onion on clean boards,
Pipe sugar into battleships. My guide, the chef,
Stares with impunity, steals from their hoards

Even crisp, green pea-pods, flown from France,
So time is frozen, April tastes July.
He seizes Danish pastries next, which lie
Glinting their snow and cherries. We advance
Past sausage rolls and vats of coughing soup
To the cool shelves, where spices breathe in jars;
His private stores — Sienna honeycake —

A gem, a feast. But not the real meal
Which weighs me like a stone. It is too hot,
I long to go and lie on a cool floor.
I think of the bare kitchen which I saw
Scrubbed, quite abandoned. Now the students pass
Outside; to sprawl untidily on lawns,
Chew through packed lunches; nibble stalks of grass.

Toad

Stretched on the road, spread like a hand,
One leg crawling, behind him — I swerved. I was thinking
Of resignation: how I hated
Wet, Friday nights. Now this dead frog:
But it was a toad. As I scooped him out blackness
His pale fingers opened; breath sucked in his sides
He was swollen with anger. He had been crawling
Close to the gutter, in fury of rain
Trusting its stream.

     And where was his pond?
The scoop by the willows the builders were filling?
There is water in one of the horses' fields
In winter, a flood; in summer, a glimmer.
But not to be found in the dark. He was cased
In a high plastic dome, a tray of plants
Sweet Williams or wallflowers; having for water
A plastic dish; and a stone; where he crouched
With only his gold-rimmed nose, still sucking.

I wanted him. What need to be
A prince; with eyes of rusty gold
And brightest black? If I had ponds
With subtle lilies, I would keep him.
But next day, he began to leap
Purposed, silent, launching up
On high back legs — then falling back
Banging the dome, his hidden sky.

We took him through the floating grass,
He was not resigned. Given his stone,
He leapt straight out, splashing and stirring
Dangerous flood, to open sky.
(Two ducks flew, squawking, by our heads.)
He settled then, to his new mud;
His olive back in the drowning grass
His gold eye to the feckless air.

Is he still there? I would not say
That toads are happy, good, or fond
Of their own place; but go for miles,
Choosing their mud, finding their mate,
Until the water glazes ice,
The heron finds the pond.

The slow train

He was in the dark train coming home from London
The train which waits in sidings, shakes from Swindon
In the cold smell of dust, the gleam of half-lit mirrors.
He looked at none of them for past or future
But stretched in the seat opposite
His heels found his kitbag, marked
With frequent names in stencilled white.
His hand slipped from the silver bag
Which held dress uniform, or some
Loved private clothing. And he slept.
Until the lights shook him awake

Until some thousand miles of sea
Rushed under him. Until the rock
Jarred under boots. From the slow train
I see the half-mown hayfield, bare
In shaven earth, scraped dusty red.
Inside the dirt-streaked window's glare
His face shakes, quickly, the long dead.

Cook's

Standing in the travel agent's queue
Since Istanbul has not replied — Corfu
Has no double beds left — thirstily
I drink the posters.
                Smoke of sea
Rises to my mouth. The milky towers
Are Trebizond, lie too far east for safety:

They do not exist. Though there are people
Who will smile at us and tell us lies
Spot our dyed hair, our trustful eyes,
No one should sell us hopes.
                  I do not leave.
I shuffle forward in the snaking queue
Wait, as one too knowingly deceived,
Being — somewhat — in this business too.

Now

Now you are real,
the curve of your back
your voice in my hair:
how the metal of work
has scarred your long fingers with shadow

see, my slow fingers are stretching,
dark wires singing, I choose you.

Now you are real. I can lose you.

Places

The wood whose paths still steamed, which turned
Wednesday to a breathing cave of rain
Whose trunks barred light, flickered my forehead,
Unaware and tender as a hand
May be to someone else the place they quarrelled
Never to enter in again
May be, to the unseen bird, home:
Neither beautiful nor strange —

A room with a curved window, in which Dover
Rises a rim of hills, woods yellow, green;
Below, shows sea's sharp rock. Next door
A black cat washes delicate, on stone;
The roofs stretch up towards us as the cat
Stretches from dark feet; the room
To someone else gives money, bread:
A room to air, a room to rent,
Out of clouded sun, to count
The blankets tangled on the bed.

News

Between lessons, he collapsed, inside a cloakroom
jamming the door fast: so when they came
He was already dead. She halts. I see him
the grey suit wrinkled, like an elephant:
His eyes wide open. All we ever said
to hustled day, blue whisper of a moon
was, how cold it is! and will it snow?
She tells me his wife died a year ago;
I guess, then, that he crumpled, worn by sorrow.
Nothing is as simple. She says soon
he was to re-marry; that the woman
has had her one son killed, and lives alone.

In the storeroom after she has gone
The crackled red has vanished, the faint light's
a thin, new twig: a trembling line I cannot
see as cut sharp, alone: but singled out

from dust, the moon unkindled: the dark planet.

True romance

I thought today about the girl
Who worked once with me in a shop,
Whose mouth turned down, whose fiancé
Was kind and stocky, bald on top.

She talked to him about their house,
Lace tablecloths and all its wants.
All lunchtime bit her nails, and read
Long cartoon strips of true romance.

I do not have lace tablecloths
I have compared you to the sky.
Yet in her space — which aches from both
Dark dream and day — I wake and lie.

Lady

You were buying chips for everybody, when the gipsy came.
She saw the five pound note closed in your hand,
Instead of clothes pegs, offered you a charm.
So you bought one; then for your friend, the same.
She said that you were generous, how things would come to you.
            You were a lucky lady.

You have bored children; married out of school,
Your husband half the week gets up at three
To do more overtime. But it is true,
You think more good in life than I can see:
            Lady, O lucky lady.

The glass room

The man who is dying comes to see me,
We always got on well. His face is paper-white, his eyes
Are brighter than my room.
His house is tidy. He is giving out his books.
I walk with him, to fetch a tiny box
He cannot lift upstairs. What do I say?
I tell him what I'm doing. He says 'Yes,' indulgently,
His new voice light; we always got on well.
The door swings out: soft morning. I tell him of our work,
He says it is too frantic, he is glad
He is retiring, he can go away.
As he leans into the car, careful of breath,
I lose my way. I ask about the green house
Where (he told me once) his winter freesias
Flood, with one flower's scent, a whole glass room.
Yes, he still keeps the greenhouse; not the long allotment
Where now blue winter kale would reach his knees
Where his sweetcorn blew: silk, foreign green
Which did not ripen. Now he would not care,
Be mild, be stranger. But my stone
Shatters the panes, birds circle, in still air,
Where the voice rises: quickened, harsh: his own.

Rosa mundi

It is Rosamund's rose. She is not history, but legend,
So I will lie of her with a calm face
Let all the stories tangle in my heart
As her own scarlet thread, burning the grass
Which led the jealous Queen to a leafed place
Where she sat, sewing. Great cups of flower
Flush the eager face, but you draw back
Will have none of it, useless pretty work

I know, which ate her hours; I know.

                                        I know
This rose was never — pretty. It will sprawl
Across the small dry bed, without a pole
To keep it from the wind, or sheltering wall.
Yet it will last out winter, I am sure.
Across its petals, white and purple flood,
Warm continents: as eyes: which never could
Meet. So it is planted in a place
It tangles, fights, till fresh leaves arch, stroke space.

Weather

Each path is filled with water
Each rut blinks white.
Clouds scud and pass on, faster
Than train. Than sight.

The guard bends for the ticket
The guard says 'Yesterday
I came from Scotland to Penzance,
The rain held all the way —'

Each path is deep with water
Beneath the blind sky's race,
Murder cracks a new heart,
The rain strokes every face.

The dealer

Can you see through his window? There is so much dust —
It is not on the glass; it is breathed from the things;
The long-stemmed glasses with their heavy cuts
The fire-irons, their plating flamed with rust
The plaster angels under snow-chipped wings,
All valueless. As to a scent, you turn:
Something is always hidden in his place,
The small bronze dancer searching the clear air —
He may not sell her. He will scan your face.

He opens the door early in the day
All through Bank Holidays. Then shuts at noon
Though people come and rattle at the door.
Sometimes he paints a sill; at times he may
Pack boxfuls; take them back into his rooms;
The high house in a sidestreet where a floor
Collapsed once, from heaped weight. They say of him
That he is awkward, has no purposes
But hoarding; so, cannot find anything.

No, he will sell. He sold me the first jug
Saying how cheap it was, that it is old
Although it shows no mark. And I believe him,
It has a white snake, crawling to the rim
Stilled in a handle. Snakes are surely old.
He fetched a lustre jug out of his rooms
Because I liked it. Yes, he did
Strange things for me. I know those eyes
Pale, not unkind; which show no lid;
He could find each thing in his shop
As I can see books in my room
Without a light, close eyes; stroke bark
And know the tree. Jugs crack — We should
Love people who take nothing from the dark.

The row

I could not stand up to her:
Her pupils' wide, unseeing stare
Did not alarm you. So you won.
But all day I have thought of her
In the sun's shadow, the frost's glare
I move in what I held too near:
The beast's patience. The beast's fear.

Bookkeeping

These are not (you understand) the figures
which send cold judgement into the backbone
which leave us, workless, shrunk at home
staring in a sky grown black with leaves.

These are like the ticking of a clock,
the daily sums, a van's new brakes,
three drums of trichloroethylene on the back
of a thrumming lorry; yet they take
a day to make: thin bars of figures. While
I try to balance them, light scurries round
like a glad squirrel. Radio music stales —
until shut off.

        What's left when it is done,
the green book closed? There is no sea to swim
no mouth to kiss. Even the light is gone.
Bookkeepers drink over-sugared tea
lie in dark rooms; are always hunched and tired.

Where I stretch up the low bulb burns and whirls.
And in it, I see him. The dusky gold wing folds
across his face. The feathers' sharp tips smudge
his margins.

sunk, in his own shadows, deep
in scattered ledgers of our petty sins:
he, the tireless angel:
Unaccountably, he sleeps.

II

Horses

Flowers

Homecoming

Horses have quick routes they know
A few safe roads, on which they always go,
They are not tempted by the sudden lane
The silver poplar shivering in light.
They only crave heaped hay again,
And pull to keep the low white yard in sight.

So I must fight them, if I am to go
On fruitless roads, on past the dulling tree;
Nor could I tell them, even if I knew
What it was we turned so far to see,
Before the hungry stables of the night.

Hill mist

I am too fond of mist, which is blind
without tenderness; whose cold clings close
round the face.

The timid horse likes it;
treading his own space,
he cannot see black haystacks loom
the dog wait in wet woods; the man
crouch in brambles, raise a gun,

Even its sound is muffled. Death would be quiet in the mist.

Up on the crest — though you will say
he bucks, he gallops — how calm you seem
rising soundlessly over the grass.

Mist lets you in — All I see are the dancing
lights advance: evaporate.

The mist grows into a strange horse
the slender chestnut mare — the solid man, we saw
once riding with a woman; always, now, alone.
You make as much of this as the white shapes
smoke, in my eyes — All I will say
is, he is hard, as ground is: in bravado
rides bareheaded. How the mist must cling
to him. As you step out, our horse's mane
hangs heavy, dewed and glinting:

There is no past here. The only future's
The hidden gallop's heat. It is a place
I did not mean to love. Do you live so:
Walking your own space?

Breaking out

Pinto is out again! He kicks his door
Till the bolts give. Last time he only wandered
To the trough to gulp the freezing water
Then back into his stall. But now he bursts
Bristling to the cold, bright black and white
Through all of us, across the radiant yard.
The stablegirls run shouting. Ros
Has found the camera — Ros is young and shy,
Like a thin tree: her teeth caught in a brace,
Pale hair bunched down her spine; and all she loves
Is horses. 'I must catch him —' Not with hands;
She has her own horse: chestnut, fine-boned, staring
As a magpie head sweeps past his door.
Feet clatter ice — it's not her own she wants —
Pinto is out! The boy sent to pile snow
Across their road, warning of six foot drifts
In the next hollow, looks up — hurls a spade
As Pinto wheels, straight through the open gate
Across the unwalked white which was the field.

The stable girl falls stumbling in a drift
But Pinto's prints, triumphant, leave a curve
As planes track a clear sky: and the sky lifts
Great, blue, unshadowed. Knee-deep in the drifts
He canters, skips, snow-shod. A while, he stops,
Scuffing his nose white, sniffing. Ros and I
Press against the wire in ice-blue shadow.
'Take him now!' I say. 'Too near,' she wails.
He plunges out of focus. He comes near
To eye my brandished carrots, meant for Glen,
Nearer, nearer. I do not want him caught.
I feel her shoulders tense, squinting at each
White step: a photograph, a means: the end
The strange eyes shining, always, out of reach.

Snowbound

The horses skidded on the black-iced road
Stiff-legged as skiers, snorting the raw air.
The sheep and lambs lay quiet in the fields,
Bundles of grey, against the miles of snow.
Hock-deep, the horses floundered through the gate
Mistrusting the steep track they used to know.

Blue, the tall young hunter, climbed ahead
Breasting the drifts, tossing and plunging deep.
The soft snow caved around him, poured and echoed
A dull white thunder on the icy hill.
So my horse stiffened, fumbling in the craters:
The small grey pony? Can he manage? Still

Charging the slope, below the drifts, on hard
Horse-trodden snow, he scrambled up behind
His mane gold-glinting, like a dandelion,
Against such brightness, bristling at the cold,
He came, fastest of all, and his eyes shone.

Blue stumbled in a dip, sank to the chest.
'We can't go through,' his rider called. To that
The file fidgeted: Paddy, the best
At jumping, and the grey horse who will pull,
Run off for miles — whipped down sudden heads
Into blue-shadowed folds, to sink, to roll.

Their frightened riders tugged their reins up hard,
Swung round — What had they seen? No earth, no grass —
They had been stabled now for months — what glare
Or perfect promise in the glittered field?

We edged back down our path, left snow's loud falls behind,
Hooves scraped off the firm road. 'Horses are mad!' we said,
Miles out, from heat and home, out in the high, east wind.

March night

The road streams, to the moon. The sky
Is green and solid, lapped by light
The stars are buds, leaf-furled and white.

The children clatter out of dark
Pushing down the stable cart.
'Don't crash it, like you did last night!'

My horse licks out my feeding hand
Stares at the upturned cart, diverted:
The slow moon climbs, behind his head.

As the spilled children pause for breath
Above the broken bread and apples,
Across the sudden fields, sound bells.

I never knew bells which have been
Tumbled, mad, and very sweet
Cast seed so, through a sky's cracked green.

Riding: Easter

I saw her fall
Roll across the rough ground, crying out,
The stirrup, torn from saddle, flash and lie
Beside her. As my horse and I swerved past,
In the mad downhill rush I did not see
The young horse fail to clear her, kick her twice
Till blood ran down her face, she lay back, still.

Fighting with horse and ground to miss a tree
I felt us stagger, stumble, I was down
With nothing but an arm of nettle stings
And a red scrape across one cheek to show;
The child who fell, pride lost, who ran up crying,
Whose stiff small back I rubbed — oh, none of this
Matters, though it happened. But the man
The quiet-voiced man from London asked me who had fallen,

Realising: he thrust his reins at me,
Said 'my wife — oh Jesus —' stumbled, forcing
Through molehills, banks of nettles. Bright and small
They stood, the circle of the puzzled horses
Round a silence blowing quiet to
The shaking girls who set the tumbling pace;
Around: the great trees, and their shade, but he
Crouched in the sun, cradled her broken face.

Grooming

Mud hangs its dry beads on your eyelid,
Not on red and glossy hair, but the dark skin
Too tender to be brushed. I hesitate
And then I lick the sponge and touch it to you.
You sigh with pleasure, slip your heavy head
Into my other hand: and let me rub.
Stepping round, stroking your ears, I think
We are too narrow, and our labels
Far too few.
All the loves and all the warmth shut out —
The yard is empty. Finished, like this horse
Who on the hill-top cries for his own kind —
How suddenly, intensely, I want you.

Staying at Coberley

As we talked, beside a window dimmed
With corn dust, I could see the dark shape hurtling —
My horse, in the strange paddock, crashing round
Storming nettles, clouds of May's cow parsley —
He was brought to spend the night, so we might borrow
Their horse, to go out through the cool of morning.
There were creatures everywhere: her little dogs
Who pattered in while we were soaping tack
Who blinked at us, each one a different colour;
The hen, half-pet, half farm's, bustling the chicks
Down corridors of stables.
                                    Half the night
I watched his shadow flash the clouded glass.

But he was quiet, in the morning's rain
He walked to us under the sycamores
Dripping with yellow flower. We rode for miles;
He licked the white mare's neck; but now we go
Through steaming woods, back to the plain, known stables.

Purple smokes in trees' shadows: bluebells, close,
Tempting to pick. Already he is staring
Back at the farm, sunk in its grassy dip —
I have not seen it under snow — he mourns
The white mare, summer's creature; will be quiet
Next week—
                        I am afraid. How habit hangs
And clings to hands: cool bitter juice of bluebells.

June 21st

I hear you moving softly on the stairs
I rise to follow; it is almost dark;
After the long ride, I smell it, sharp,
The scent of horse on my own skin, as sweet
As their green mouth-froth; grass and seed; a flare
Of speed which does not look, I recognise:
Yet fought today, until my stretched arms ached
'Pull *up*!' The green ground flows — the cliffs end there.

Summer and night — I would ride there again
Washed by rank sweetness of the elderflower
Whose huge, green plates are curled, buds still; to break
To moons. How bare, how high, moons will rise there
Nor show the stones in deep grass, till too late.
No night is safe: but how to hold the light

Escapes you, also? Grounded: I must slide
Lean on the horse's damp hard neck and feel
Us separate. This is the longest day.
Up on the land's green shoulder, barley-sleek
The lovely red-brown of my arms could stay
Close to the sun. Cooler: come home: I lie
Where the grass blows longest, dock seeds, finest,
To thread the sky; a gold snail climbs, its shell
A tiny sun. The stable-cat comes, to rest.
I lift my face up to her; see the sky
Veined with a trace of cloud which does not move,
Feathered with one trail; soft silvered, steel,
The long sky of day's ending: the slow west.

One bare day, will I work? I, who do not believe
In happiness, wake, keeper of small keys,
Reader of books, a rider
Of no man's horses? You my night
I need no hands to touch now: I call moons
To marvel at you, flood your silent gates,
I follow you. Under enormous sky
The horses sleep, together, without sight.

Saddle-sore

You always galled me. First, the glossy hair
and then the pale skin
which never properly mends. Again, this spring
it opened and half-healed, shows whitening hair
around the dull red scab, dark as a jewel,
the blood, just sealed.
                                        We are not stone.

But if you were the saddle, and I rode
— my pain; the creaking leather —
could I not forgive you, even love you?
Still, in some lights, it does not seem too late.

Meanwhile, I wander, round the tiny field,
and do not lift my head to hear the gate.

Cheltenham races

It is a cold business. I have seen horses, under
The headlong rain, sprawled on its wet ground, lying
With leg or back past help; no longer trying
To rise: one ear pressed in the torn grass
Till the gun's shout. Are we then, kinder
To people? the small men in wheelchairs
Spin aside to watch the horses pass,
Still pale, alert and shrunk, they were once jockeys.

Quick winnings — yesterday's — a night's wild poker
Warm Irish travellers in slow ticket queues.
Remote and blue, cigar smoke licks round us.
Upon the skyline's hill a new warmth blows
From twigs where dark buds thicken and thrust higher.
Heads dip, quick waves of light above the crowd:
The horses. A white tail glints, it flows
In the parade ring's air. A silvered braid

Twists through the severe plaits of the girl
Who leads her hard-legged bay. He halts, the best:
But I watch the light grey: as all the rest
Bound on the bit to start, he turns to stare
Up in the humming sky which bends on him.
All curve through my binoculars, slow whirl
Of silks and backs, becoming something else:
The grey comes out of line, brushing through hurdles,
Eyes staring, pulling, pounding, into darkness —

A huge elbow rears up: it fills my sight —
They flicker back with light on the long hill.
The grey lags, now, the bay swings smoothly, will
Lead at the turn. Then I lose the last fence,
With forests of hats, hoarse shouting — Who is down?
Grey neighbour rips his ticket. The winners slow, they jog
Riders raise muddy goggles stare back:

                              he is still lying,

The great bay. There they stand
Ambulance men, a jockey, his thin girl
Who led him round — As we stand: quiet: he stirs,
Heaves to his feet, then shakes. At once, we cheer
Shuffle torn tickets, seeing the scarlet rug
Smoothed along his back — He walks through us
Slowly to stables; down the littered slope
Watched, warm as winner, led still by the silver,
Which glints in a girl's hair: old folly, hope.

Arks

You should be cleaning. I should be typing lists,
Stock checks. Instead: propped on the storeroom's sink
We talk for hours. The others fidget. Glimmered fish,
One, tabby cat, keep them well satisfied.
You have two children; six dogs. We decide
How long a Belgian Shepherd's tail should grow.
Do we want Persian cats? Or should I strain, to buy
The great bay hunter with the Roman nose?

You are in danger. Passion in your eyes,
Surrounded by the warm wind of the beasts —
All your children's days out are to dog shows.
For you, with rough paws dangling from each chair,
For me, dipping my face in gold-tipped fur
Feeling the black mane toss to trot, how long:
Before we turn, and see the unscrubbed sink,
The water rising; and the people, gone?

Port Meadow

Upon the common ground beside the river
The grass is thin. The horses, owned,
But ridden rarely, picked a living
Among tall poisonous ragwort and the brittle
Singing stems of nettles.
                                        Till she came
In a flapping mackintosh, with bales
Of hay, with barley rustling in its bags.

At first she fed them, named them, stood with them
As though to guard them. Then she moved
Into the clumsy hut, left from the war.
She slept in its wet dark. She was as clever
As all the mad are, was indeed, a scholar;
To mark the Finals, walked through town; the rough
Coat above the long black of her gown,
As the silk grain whispered in her cuffs.

Horses keep herds for safety. Down that winter
They stood together silent through the nights
With ice thick on their manes, their tails tangled
In the east wind: breathing a warmth which then
She lost; beneath her and the canvas bed
An empty stove; a half-filled bag of grain.

Did the herd miss her, moving up the stream
Stretching stiffly, in the glow of morning?
I think they did. Though I am not more fond
Of animals than people; yet the giver
Of food is loved, as they would live,
                                        I leave
A cold bed, almost envious, to reach
Their solid breath; beside the smoking river.

The Staffordshire horses

Were bought at different times; are not a pair,
The first was claimed as eighteenth century
And charged as such, specially obtained, and rare.
The second turned up cheaply; it appears
Similar; but moulds were used for years;
What's 'genuine'? As waves lift, bare and strange,
The lines which drew me to them do not change.

But you have not seen them. The horses pace,
One foreleg raised. The riders are both men
One has a sword, one not. They are smooth-faced,
Blank as soldiers. Their cloaks sweep, and meet
Curves of the horses' bellies, snowy feet.
They are all white; as if light spilt
The flanks are speckled, dusted down with gilt.

And both are still unwrapped. We have not found
Any shelf or window-ledge so high
No cat may spring up, brush them to the ground.
I must try again; must make somewhere
They can pace, apart and like, above,
Switch on a sudden light, to find them there
Plain and dazzled; strangely starred as love.

Horse-dealing

I am wondering whether to buy you:
you are much too strong for me
snort up the heavy ploughland
mud-splashed, a dragon, slide
to smoking halt; dance sideways out on cliffs —
undaunted, still survive
while eating more than any horse
I ever knew; can rip bare gorse
from brushwood fences. Yet the sense
I hold of you, is something else:
checked on the cold hill-path, you gaze ahead
your speckled ears sharp to catch the space
of tiny woods; crouched hills, your nose
cream as the brimmed meal-bins, lifts pale
to the great winter light. Through which I race
to someone too, in love with distances
who is — no more than you — for sale.

Stone horse

She is two; with small eyes which see everything.
I like her, as I fear her. She is harder
Than the hundred students in a room
Whom I keep quiet with ease. For she is quiet:
But purposeful. She crosses our rough grass
Where honeysuckle trails, dusked purple, where
The sly fritillaries, blue-leaved like grass,
Watch her with their snake's eyes. She stands by the stone horse.

I stroke its ears, its cream and lavish mane
The collar round its neck — a unicorn's.
She peers into its chiselled face and sighs,
Stoutly impressed. 'Can it open its eyes?'

They are carved open; but in pale stone:
Would she believe those brilliant, icy pupils
The Greeks painted on gods? Or does she think
The head will turn: blinking and bright: alive?

I bend, confused. For I want many things.
'You do not understand. It is just stone,
Come down the road, to see my real horse.'
Or fairy stories. 'When you are asleep,
It gallops through the grass —' You are too good
For such deceit. You felt speed prick its ears;
Shadow quiver, breathe its nostrils, as I did.
You beg to sit astride.

How chill it is
In April's summer. For I sit there too
Blinking in autumn sun, drinking my coffee
Watch something, in its haze. I do not promise, now
A miracle, our hardness will unfreeze
That the stone horse should see — I am about
To take you, kicking protest, to your mother,
Betray you. I say: 'Maybe.'

All untrue,
Those eyes shall open: when you want them to.

Night Visit

We are ridden — he said — by the ghost
Of a lost authority.
There are mistakes,
I shall not make;
I shall not throw flowers
Under the hooves of the centaurs of power.

The snow, which rustles roofs,
Has all the horses stir,
The wild pony beats
A hard hoof on the door.
There is a dream from which
I do not ask escape:
A dream, whose haunting shapes
The snow on half-lit air.

We cannot shake off ghosts:
We cannot run so fast
Only the perfect snow
Has no first or last.
I cannot see, if my horse
Watches above the door.
In this scraped, sudden air
No one has passed before.

Sunday morning

The horse eats everything. Cow parsley; white dead-nettle,
Young hawthorn sprays and — afterthought — the grass.
A dandelion spins sideways from his lips
As he looks up and chews. Down his rough mane
The quick sun slides
                              it pierces our slow mist
My skin glows in its thick cloth and the horse
Shrugs a red shoulder, rubs his head on knees
Brushing the first fly. He snuffs the path,

His nostrils are as eyes. They open wide,
Over the ancient droppings, horses' marks,
They shiver, read, pass on. I drop the reins
And watch the paths of silver down the field
Crushed grass, a tractor's tracks. The light walks lines of silk
Between thin branches, broken as we pass.
What use is it, this sun? It is not human
It would not know your face or where you went
But in the cold ditch, floods your eyes with warmth:
Gold without coin, unconsumed, unspent.

The Chinese horse

A neat receipt declares 'Late Ming':
That horse was never late, for anything,
Could gallop great, grey marsh all day and pull
All the way home — watching the herons fly
Like sparrows. Leaves' warmth opens in its dull
Green, yellow glaze. Its head thrusts to a sky
I could not bear. Its mouth curls. Should I own it?
The young man, stained and pale as ivory
Disapproved. 'If you wish to re-sell —'
Rugging the flanks with paper — 'we will buy it.'
He called it 'little chap'. Its empty eye
Said nothing. In some packing case, rolled ship,
An ear's tip broke to dust. The saddle's scarred,
It bears no rider. While, today, I fetch
The photographs of us with the red horse:
His tilted, heavy head; the pony's feet;
A coat brushed rough from mud. His eyes shine out
Lazy with autumn sun. And I: too stiff
With crooked smile, with shadowed eyes, advance
From frames at blurring trot; against a wind
I feel alive, but which is turned
Upon me. Twenty years — the red horse gone —
Fifty years — The strong back's still; not mine
The gold, glazed saddle, and the rider, time.

Advice

'Come then: to conclave. I have brought the food —
Baked hard in the oven — which you love:
Now, as your stall is open and set near
The new grey pony with the muscled neck,
Pinto the piebald, quick and sharp as paint
Brandy, who charges first up every hill —
Then I must feed you all. How is the bread?'

'Too soft, too white: you should have left it longer.
Now — we suppose — you mean to talk of him,
With nothing left to chew at? Brandy's stamp
Says everything. Tell us: when did he take you
Up to our hill, where beech leaves smell of pepper
Shine orange, smooth as leather, where the blackbird
Bursts like a bomb, out of the underwood —
When did he take you there?'

'Not recently:
He stays too much in rooms.'

'Then he is patient
As we, beneath the brush, our eyes half-closed,
Hoof resting, nostrils shivering with pleasure —'

'I do not recognise that patience.'

'No? You need advice. Take us, as solid
As roads which steam with morning; if we run
It is all quite explicable; the gate
Had not been painted yesterday —'

                                      'You take
My mints and apple. What have I for him:
How shall I bribe him: conscience? What he thinks
Is cold: with future. Will your warmth hold instead?'

'Future?' They yawn, a long time: narrow eyes,
Arch long tongues. The worn, pale gold teeth close:
They cross my palms. 'Why have you no more bread?'

Welsh Song

Glen, small, bay horse: since I complained
Of your short name, we have devised a long
New title to which you may trot in time;
Glendower, quick, red horse, I will give you a Welsh song.
First we will declare that you are not
The dark racehorse whose shoulder I just touch
Who eats the hill in seven strides; or such
A brave white mare as Martha, whose great trot
Called to the morning streets through which I rode.
You are bored by walk and circling, in the covered school;
Will you lighten, if I take you to the hill,
Where, cantering this day, you sprang aside,
Tore past the others, flattening corn? and still
Shaking, on safe paths I vowed to have you.
Through the high Welsh summer, I rode a small black mare
Who loped her heather like a cat, dodged through
The dripping woods, all ease — To take you there —
Would that be Paradise? Yet she had, too
Her terror: one car, crawling the hill, sent her
Scrambling the bank, through pigeons, wet gold moss.

That was a strange company — the dentist's English wife
With her light voice and her young careful hair,
Pleading boredom, riding with a college friend
A slim man, going grey. And yelling, everywhere
Galloping — the wild girl off the farm
Whose quiet sister waded, in the leaf-dark stream,
Which gave their water, which was running low:
Brown fingers cleared the pipe, searched out the source:
So in red rains, past heat of engines, we
Will see your quick land run, Glendower my horse.

Aims

As water bursts up through the frozen road
I must remember, suddenly,
How I once planned to live, alone,
Funded for ever by some vague success —
The rest glowed clear. The sheltering field
With the slim mare I rode each day,

Through woods I planted; grey wolfhounds
To heap my bed, growl safety by my fire.
I live as you do; hedged around
By people, traffic, washing, bounding higher
Than fences; horse — one mile away. To find
His keep, others will ride him. Could we stand
That loneliness: to own our heart's desire?

Paradise song

Were there queues, also in Eden? For virtues? No repeating?
My red and solid pony stayed elsewhere. Eating.

Did they, there, hand duty down? visit your family,
Bear two children, keep the world on course —
I stood at the winds' gate, talking with a horse

Who snuffed the scent of apple. As it blew,
The queues dispersed, dear reader. Where were you?

Breeding

I had suspected it; from that fine white
Flash of the eye as he swings up his head
Which called back horses flinging over paddocks
Hauled down by labelled stableboys: a shock
Of white, as a full moon rears, overhead
Her wide sky grey-green, luminous — it might
Be metal; then a sea of risky colour
Swims round her. Prudent men stay in. Moon-led,
Out in the windy yard, I look, I linger.

So, when I led him softly down the road
When the great digger rattled up behind
He dragged me, on my scraped knees, after him —
Cleaning the saddle; I asked about his breeding,
That half which is not cob. 'I think you'll find,'
Debbie said airily: 'It's thoroughbred.'
What I love most; most fear: horses who flare
Who turn with no survival in their hearts
As headlong, powerful, as the senseless air.

I squeeze the muddy sponge. As the worn leather
Is grained, we're caught in it, the risky blood.
I do not believe in purity.
I have seen my horse's eyes: luminous, misty
Their centre blue as flowers — then black; opaque as flood.
Should I have bought him? But I was not warned,
Now I am caught by love, and no more free
Than the strong hand, which drags us to be born.

Joshua

I

It is July. I drive, looking for a man
Who has been 'all kinds of things'; now keeps six horses
Behind the hillside of tall Council flats.
Thunder crackles at the edges of the land.
I have wondered, would it frighten horses
To plunge at each crack; or stand shivering, as
Joshua will; head dropped, by the blue rushing train?
Are there parts of our own towns which frighten us?
In this town, it's the statued, sloping parks
Where blind gangs come; or out of laurelled rain
Someone steps, in tall, unseeing streets.

Here no one misses anything. We crowd upon an island:
As in the flats, named after a princess
Now, a grandmother. How young, the mothers
Wielding their prams — hard to tell the boys, who stand,
Chase footballs on the battered no one's grass
From those who walk by wives, are now the others.
A girl from here you taught: too shy: whose parents parted,
Liked you. Driving me, you pointed. 'There she is.'
Flying round a corner, tall on an old bike. Lorna,
Seeing no one, keeps her shy mouth parted;
Alone in silence: brief and blind as thunder.

II

When I first saw you, I was terrified.
You swung your head, each eye ringed with fine white.
I looked down the neck's slope, the hard dark line
Of leg, stamping the rough planks. Thoroughbred —
So tall, he helped to throw me in the seat
Of the ancient saddle where I hunched
And felt you stumble stiffly down the road.

'Josh is quiet,' he insists. I do not believe, till there
In the ruts and nettles of the field
I pull gallop back to canter, in my fear
Jerking, cruelly hard. But he will give
Until the ponies storm ahead, he cries
To be with them, a sudden tearing whinny.
He springs and lengthens. I am riding air

The ground's devoured. He would pound for miles
Lengthening, breathing. This is how he won:
Till he went lame, his legs were fired,
A painful burning which destroys
Something in the leg; cannot be done again.
Then he caught harsh horse 'flu, turned skin and bone.
Now he is sleek, eats anything. He steals

Great blooms of hay from horses either side.
'When I had him first, for weeks he showed
No feeling, he was like a block of wood.
He likes me now — for food.' Where did he win?
A hand sweeps up the tall neck. 'Everywhere.'
On our next ride, a blast of rain-cold air
Met him at a small ditch. He stopped, head lowered.
Trotting back, it was agreed — for all his height,
Faced with any jump, he is a coward.

III

The white Lippizaners dance their ring. What are they to do
With the tall flats, Joshua, with us?
Fairytale — their bridles glow white silver,
Riders raise black, cockaded hats, and through
A minuet the horses sidle, go
In pairs — calmed stallions — wheel and pirouette;
A clockwork, childish past we must forget?
So I once felt Vienna, in the slow
Green crawl of canals; the coffee, slimed by cream
Pleasure soured by thunder. Yet what years

Of work shine here: that horse is twenty-three
Who on his trainer's long rein, seems
To move in the obedience of a dream.
I see bones move, in brushed skin's gleam. I see

In that most lovely pace, the pausing trot
In which feet step, like music on dark air,
I see the dream: to have time tremble there
Yet grant its wildness, to let
The stallions on a white rein, leap and fling
Strong hind feet, snorting, soaring. Then press near
For sugar from the breeches pocket. Here
Finale: slow white line, the airy trot,
As breath would hold, the wave would pause; in one
Would take us; all our terrors melted, gone.

IV

I am told that I may take you on your own
But you look back, break wheeling from the gate,
He has to catch your bridle, pull you through.
As we trot on, you call, dark shuddered shouts
For all the others, for the hay, for home;
Whirling, backing, you will not go through
The crossing gates which take you the wrong way.
The crossing man is frightened. I slide off, lead you;
                                        wonder how
I will ever reach that high back. But — one strange spring — I do.

You canter slowly down the puddled tracks,
Pass, without desire, the bucking mare
Racing her foal across the stranger's field.
We turn; you let a train pass; go demure
Across the rails, contented, going back.
I wish to turn, to see where a path leads.
You roll your eyes, back from me. I am sure
You are not frightened. I wrench round your head

Hit you, as he said, twice. You sigh; you canter on,
Lightly, to a dead end. Have I won?

Do the Lippizaners fight? I shrink from power:
Is it needed? I too, live by habit
Frightened of a street in a small town,
Shiver and flinch, as you do from the ditch,
I, from children's blinding faces — Lorna
Flying in her space. But you have woken,
It is your last stretch, and you bound the grass
Become the rush of dark, the marvellous horse.
Sweet instinct overrides fear; it is flying
The wind behind us, we are the air's thunder
The path casts up low willows. Without check
Rain, silver leaves lash at our eyes: but you
Ride earth. I press my face to your damp neck.

Mr Street

He praised your shoeing, then your ease
In riding; said, as you were seventy-three,
That you were selling all the horses up.

Gone: as stars scatter. Now I see
Why you worked so hard on me, to buy
Martha, half Irish drayhorse, who would stand
By shuddering buses like a rock; and my
Beloved Joshua; dark, springing horse
With fine and ruined legs. You even tried
Tall Brandy, who could buck me to the sky,
But had him safely sold to someone else.

You were a rescuer. The wilful mare
Who, because a bit had chipped her teeth
Fought every bridle, let you slide hers on.
You had a stout brown pony, thirty then,
Whom you 'kept meaning to put down', but always
Went on; and on. The pied New Forest pony
Hobbled your paddock upon swollen feet
You daubed with healing tar. Who will buy them?

But it is true, the work was heavy. I
Remember as you led them for a ride
After the catching, shoeing, grooming — what
Strange sweat lay on your brow: like a sharp dew
Silvered: a warning. So you heard at last
Your heart's complaint, to outlive horses. Yours

I've heard you number, like a liturgy.
Jumbo, Pepper, Candy, Topper, Patch —
You talked fast as you rode. Can your yard be
Empty? Is your house dark? They have not
Gone. They stand, behind your shoulder. See.

III

Breaking Ground

I

Visit

It is no use pretending

this place does not exist;

or saying

there is nothing noble here:
which is true: it is the bottom of the world
the grey sea-bed, where the quick fishes gleam
and turn away. And were there others, once?
we feel, there should be bones: but mud has eaten them.

This place remains too mean to love the dead
or any living thing
admits the day
as pressure of thick water on the forehead —
we do not think to breathe again. Despair
lies several fathoms up. By it, perhaps,
by evening you'll have risen to the dune,
unlooked for as the dead, whose wiry grass
bent dark to wind, scribbles the sand. Down here,
even in this dark, I feel it root:
more beautiful, more sad, than women's hair.

Door's locked. Begin. She yawns,
she has not combed that hair:
I am neater — dead, so unsurprised,
but wish her lovelier as women were,
Mary: young and clear: Patty's long mouth
the gold and broken light across her eyes,
my wide land gone. I tell you who have come
Now all my words are torn, to write me down:

they make porridge here — I sleep; they give me food,
more than the hungry world. My windows tremble iron, my name's
not yours or for your purposes:
                    and each day it will change

                        But ask for grace
who I was, might be: though in my place,
cold as waters froze my roots, you came.

The room spreads — bare as silence — a small table
At which you sometimes write. You face me now:
And I am startled, first, that you are able
To turn so young, lit sudden as a fire
Smile dark — tree shadows glide on boards below.
What ground: what roots are yours? What stubborn glow?

Even to the dark my land would shine:
sharp-rimmed with gold as sun outlines a cloud —
then light soaked through its soil, flowed down each line
to the plough's blade; rising, glittered, showed
horses' clipped manes, warm turning flanks, slow steam;
cracks in the skin of leather: love
was lit in small things, I believed,
the goldfinch tossing tiny in the wind
the kingcup's yellow splash by flooding stream.

In winter we ran headlong to the cold
which numbed our fingers quickly; we would leap
on great sheets of white along cart-tracks
to feel the ice crash, the black water break
gurgling and free. The frost-ruts stubbed our toes.
Hare and hounds we played through parishes,
stumbling home through dark, saw none too soon,
bright as our scraped plates, the famished moon.

So I was bound upon the seasons' wheel.
And truly, I do not remember pain

except of falls; unworried hunger; then
I did not have to plan. The sun, so new,
a miracle to slant my sleep, became
familiar: dull and weary as a drum,
beats endless winter I cannot turn from.

II

'Still young'

'Consciousness,' she says, cold and straight.

I cry,
Never use those words to me again:
paradox, paradigm, unconsciousness,
what light can such raise, flicker warm between us?
the world is dead enough before my eyes.
I had words once, which touched the quick in bone —
hunger, love, kind, cold, say those again —

why do you stare? You're young still. I
grow wise, grow stranger, since I died.
I took cold coin from others' lips,
wearied, as the sun I told you of,
my lark's tongue, now shot with lead,
You shall not cheat —
the lark's eye gleams, your hand aches heat,
scrawl quick: be true. When I am gone
you can tear all, as my dividing head
Is split with light. But now, go on,
Look from your page: to eyes. Why come to me?

I did not wish to speak. To quick eyes — I
Who thought only to listen, must reply.
The wind is huge. It is the leaves' last day:
undersides moth-white, they darken panes:
outside, they leap like creatures from my feet
but creatures hide from wind. The field-mouse, warm,
sleeps in its grass-ball, shivering. Air beats
the swan into the bank. Woods lift. Sky sweeps away
clouds grey and bright as birds; the cliffs blur, bays
flinch blue; the sunlight of all Africa;
and in the perfect Polar light new snow

drives and stills, smooth as a sleeping face,
below, the spring's flowers. The world rocks and goes
eyeless, through the ocean of blown space
against the silence, the dark waves of air:
'I, too, come from the country, which is rarer
than in your life. I know the signs which yield
only themselves: clear red of thorn buds; starlings
whirling upwards from the planted fields:
not enough,' I tell the shadowed eyes.
'Nor you, you will not save me. Who saved you?
When did you realise those who loved you, who
worked for your books, had nothing left to teach you?
that, past sure words and head's shake, there was nothing:
but absence, and the frozen dark of eyes.'

The living should comfort. No woman I loved
had eyes as cold, as green as salt water:
you are of the sharp coast: my fenlands were warmer,
I would call back a kind wife, a favourite daughter
if either still breathed. But only the wind shakes
this glass from the metal, my mind stirs with summer

at evening, deep, in blue marsh, I had seen —
what, I forget: some migrant bird —
ran dodging, splashing the small dykes' gleam
to tell someone: I had for good, left friends:
my father hoed, at the garden's end
where the beans grew highest, bunching green
they shadowed him. Though he was tall
strong work stooped him; laid rich leaves to
knobbed hands, sunk face: there my long call
could not reach him. Fold on fold
he broke the weeds' ground; stiff; deaf to
my bird, heart's heat. I saw him, old.

'I read those stories you heard, as a child,
of witches, kind things, who came to lap cream.

My old did not tell those. They closed the dark's dreams
never having, knowing enough. They turned
to say how the cowslip wine burst in their cupboard,
golden, foaming: who married — who
quarrelled for wills, in the low grange farms.
Yet patching breaks: they said, when pay dropped low,
my great-grandmother cried to night, not knowing
how they would last to spring. I learned then, how
my grandfather, a boy, went shepherding
with his father: 'to a Show'. When they came back —
to leave the county then was vanishing,
to mapless space — as carts lurched the dark track
he saw his mother run to the top gate
her hands, bread-caked; as they heaved down the sheep,
tin trunks; black straw; she waited for the men
nor dare he run and tell her all he'd seen
where she shrank back; her long skirts floured; moth-white.

Since at the show the shepherds had damp sheds;
her husband came back coughing, lungs filled: died.
Left among the children with no more
money stored in tins, she wept; applied
to her parish for relief. The Board,
old farmers, sat behind great tables: grain
polished to dark. The rash, gold fire that roared
Shadowed their withdrawn faces, red and bored;
Inside, on a sharp hunting day, again.

They listened to her. Quickly
they said what they would give.
She said, 'That feeds the children.
But how am I to live?'
They stared back in amazement.
The fire sang beside.
'You're strong enough for work. Still young!
Woman, where's your pride?'

'The older ones can mind the younger children.'

So she went out, heaved washing, sewed.
Only half-slept, for years. Though she was strong
work has a way to bruise unseen,
so her heart surged and stopped: still young.

They were then, old enough to scramble by;
a sister washed the clothes; long-legged, they won
all the village races, left school early,
worked through the depressions; 'flitting' on
from farm to farm, on Lincolnshire's rich land;
in late years they grew heavy, settled down;
met each other rarely. They were set
firmly in the present when I knew them:
still worked all hours of daylight, would not lose
their eyes in dark, say love or wrong had been.
They slept through wars, elections; suffered; fattened
tame animals for killing:
                              never chose.'

The draughts hurl round our feet. He frowns.
                                        I praised

the chaffinch-nest, its lining, dry gold moss;
rose feathers kindling tiny eggs. And those
forgotten lives? As brave, as light as birds,
they, from me, went open to the air
unseizably. I never wrote of them.
I fought. Do not stare: cold. I will explain.

III

On the boards

I turned a boxer: although short;
with my great drive to the jaw
each time I fought I laid my man
cold, on the bare white board.

So I grew known at country fairs:
And all the boys ran after me.
Young women raised their children high
That they might turn, and see.

Then dukes and earls paid all my fare
That I might go to London,
But where I left the warm coach there
I saw a sky made stone.

In high lit rooms, I drank white wine
which let my tongue strike quick,
Cut glass rang stars, deep carpet lay
Red as my blood and thick;

but when I came back late that night,
all rooms were dark, none home.
No man I knew in all those miles
To give me bread or room

Then I walked home: and lost three fights:
and was despised by men
who fed me porridge and raw meat
To have me fight again.

But He with eyes remote as stars
Reared up to twice my size
With one great blow, He split my head
and so I sank and died.

The village shutters closed at noon.
The children, with bare feet,
to the crying of my bell
ran out along the street

   and filled the church and stood in rows
to watch the coffin pass
and on the bare and boarded box
cast every flower there was,

marigolds of sun and flame
light stocks as sweet as women's love
briar roses, frail as wrists of girls,
with every thorn plucked off —

because I faced the sun for them
and cast the dark shapes down
still they will sing me, warm and free,
though I am locked in ground.

o mad, quite mad. He had some short success,
was asked to London; treated kindly; but
nature fell from vogue; books failed; he wrote
stranger. Stranger: in and out of time
to wind and the great dark: to men's cold eyes
for whom? to no one? does he square:
Before me in this bare, white room
Torn scent, strange flowers, crowd the air.

IV

Divided

Her song

The voice I'd use to you is sure
as lover's to the day-light:
If there were no fear

(as there is always fear)

oh I would call as easily
as neighbours through the fences
If there were no quarrels

(as there are)

no singing voice but quivering,
as dusk: to the last moment
when leaves go sharply black, the sky
quick green

before stars rise

a voice you'd know in darkness:
it is sunk in you already

(as the water in the grass roots)
As the smoulder in men's eyes.

So the shadows melt in sunlight
no hard edges, pigeon colours
with the chill of stone beneath them
violet: dim blue

and the park before the children
finds the ducks in sleeping bundles
on the grass; or straggling slowly
dragging paths across the dew

while at work, the facts stay certain;
the long glass sharp-streaked by dust
as we are dying, slowly:
grow hard edges, as we must,

autumn: more deep, more wild than spring
which played cold fingers on my bones
I have forgotten wintering,
no glint of frost has touched this dress:
which now the late brief sun unfolds.
Come flow like waters on my skin,
Indias of blue and gold.

'You married only once,' I tell him, slow.
Brown fingers stroke brown wood, his table's veins,
The broad hand slams, the light wood quivers. No!

Quiet stands between us for a long time.
I hear a bird-call in white light through rain,
out in the clear day; in the fenced orchard.
I cannot hear, as you once did, the spring's
quick cry — This voice is autumn, pure and hard:
your eyes burn cold again.

Songs end. Yet I remember
what you hold out, this baffled tenderness
which would flow through the world:
but in me was divided: as it seems
even to the breaking of my mind.
For I had two wives. Mary first, then Patty.

If I say — light — what do you see? Look. Nothing?
Staring to the hawk's great wheeling sun
tore my eyes black — I sensed, half-seen from shadow
Mary, whose hands, still young
lay thin as leaves, which light might shiver through
as living flame, touch burning sky, dark trees —
so quick she came. She dazzled, baffled me:
her fingers, parting deep grass seemed to flicker.
Set free, she turned to me. We crouched, to see
close, warm-flecked eggs; May cuckoo flowers' white foam.
I trembled at her hand's glow as it touched me

how could I feel surprise when at nineteen
I reached out slowly, that she sprang away —
tugging her chilled shoulder out my hand?
shock only, at her strength.
                              Dwindling she ran
up the dusk fields: her hair, night's clouds, pale, freed.

Her father farmed on black land; wide and rich;
strange heat turned in her. Never again she ran
dark's woods to me:

                    but in neat evening's rooms
watched light bar blinds; the frost's blue flames sink: vanish

Patty's blue Sunday dress was hot, town-made;
too ruffled — till its printed yards hung foiled,
shook empty flounces through the darkening bush.
Red beads pressed to her strong throat
the thick hair slipped, from coils
dead leaves swept in its blackness as she lay:
her parted body drew me into trust
her eyes shone gold. As my low room ached day
I reached to space: I longed still for that moment
of melting where the heart grows wild, the eyes
flash dark; an end, but with no rest for me.
As with my dreams I flew, and sudden: found

110

I was woken, all my power was gone:
when fear came rushing in me — the hard ground.

Then there were others; but she grew with child,
delayed to tell me, I delayed to marry,
there were others. Yet she grew: what choice?
And so I married her and took her home,
the child due in a month; in the small room
she gasped that night for air and could not sleep,
propped on my pillow, dozed at last; by then
I could not rest. I rose. Ivy had crept
blinding the window but the full moon swept
over her hair; her hand swelled round my ring;
In the harsh flood the cheeks' flush drained to white.
I watched her face above the laboured breath:
Blanched, and black. My heart tore, for it was
My fault, not hers: who knew love: married less.

'Your seven children?' (unknown moon, swelled bright)

Still she came kind to every child. She washed,
hummed without tune, pegs clamped between strong teeth
out at the frozen line, snatched babies up like kittens.
I could love them; but how should I trust
a world so drained; so tired? How could they laugh,
run wild rings round her so?
How could she sing?

'But when they locked you up, at first, turned strange;
and you broke out and set to walk back home,
the limping miles from Essex; till they came
To fetch you with a cart —'

I remember: all of it. What then?

'Patty came with them, came to fetch you home.
How did she treat you?'

As her youngest child;
she called my name, she turned, distressed
to see me rough, and hungry. She bent strong
to lift me up again, she had not wept
but had not bound her hair up tight: it stung
in my cold eyes, black gusts,

'what did you do —'

                    ah, I broke free! I said
that here was not my wife but someone kind
I held no feeling for

                    'and yet, you wept.'

Returned: without her still. I was quite spent.
They set me in the cart, she saw me fed:
'Mary?' Birds soar, black crumbs, boards lean
to my torn feet, wheels creak;
mud's sea, glint, shine; don't take
her cry 'Six years in ground — Why ask?'

112

Strange sun, who watches everything,
still kind, she lies, I sleep. No girl
bends to me: parts the dark to grass:

Through blue, noon's sky, the planets whirl.

V

Enclosure

Look down —
you ride the cold air, as he dreamed,
but cannot rise so far
as the white mounds of cloud-floor, the high and breathless air;
that blue he dreamed: not saw.
Chill trails, low mist part round you. Peer and see
a moor; a waste; stretches of green and grey
marked by faint tracks, rough slopes where great trees stand;
small cattle, like dark grain, watched by a boy
or an old man — no hedge, wide road to break
this land of mist, space: silence. It was England
unenclosed. That space was never ploughed.
Slow in the uncut grass my skirt sweeps dark,
my feet start up deep dew. New mushrooms here
burst warm, as white as flesh — did it once seem
the fields were mine? sleep-walking as mist cleared,

I drove sharp furrows miles,
till waves of mud upon my strong boots weighed
and clogged me: but on land we worked each year.
The commons' grass was greener, tense with time,
with flowers, you could not now dream: the brief
orchids' dew-white glistening mouths. I knew
each sheltered tree; their deep roots bound my life.
To see that free land broken by the plough:
it was as if men cut my body through.

'There was a time when every elm tree died,
not in one place, but thousands. They were burned —
People took fear at it; as though the fire
which crumbled bark to ash, marked their own end.

Is there no strength in us: to ride, past change?
England lay forest once —'

You speak too narrowly.
You speak like them.

                    He kicks a rotting stump,
woodlice shower from it, over lumps
of creamy wood: they scramble, to get free.

Think what you saw: the cattle, sent to feed.
Whose were those pastures? They were common land;
all he had, that herd-boy, running down
behind a milk-cow, stamping at the cold.
The tracks lay anyone's. You walked all day
and never saw a fence. But part by part
the wild ground was divided; shut away
hedged by its owners' shadow: a rich land, without heart.

I think of building-sites, how they glow good
and warmth to winter: where the fires pull
their stubborn blue in wind: the handled bricks grow walls;
sweet through wet air you smell sawdust, dry wood.
But when smooth tiles are fixed and people come,
when builders fill their vans and disappear:
then with their shouts and roof-top whistles, gone,
strange silence rides on air:
dark, woven fences, ruffed gold flowers in rows
which are not let to mix or seed
        Enclose. Enclose.
He picks white bramble-flower clustered low
one pink — to twist them through a buttonhole.
The fruit glints black, looks sour — from frost, so soon?
He lopes, half-gipsy. Would he understand
deep towns or us: shut in them, patiently?
His light is open land.

How is your county?

'Rich,' I say, 'well-drained,
The fields are huge: skies sweep them, stunt them; now
no drifts of cowslips as my father found,
their throats splashed red; the sows live penned, inside.'

And the enclosure —

                  Once I drew its map
a child's crayon fields; remember, squelching black
unkind fruit; frosted: nothing sweet but seeds.
'The Earl of Scarborough built a carriage road —
whose cost, with hedging, fell upon all those
with any land; the poorer people sold
their ground to pay the debt. How much they owned
I cannot tell you; for they walked its measure
in strides too small for sense now: 'perches', 'rods' —'

What I arraign is not the broken mist.
We had illusions, better without them:
perhaps — Nor will I halt and name again
the plants, the paths I loved, which they destroyed.
Listen; leave that fruit. Those men did this
with shut and unkind hearts, and for their own.
What happened to those people of your village
who sold ground to meet the Earl of Scarborough's claims?
Ask your great-grandmother, broken: young. But you —
whose eyes are blurring in the glow of mist —
I know your cities. They are fortresses.
They shut out light and care. Round all of us
there is a poorer world than England was
your open world — Behind your painted doors
you hide: and all you spare falls less,

116

than scraps, we fed to pigs. Unclosed as day
my torn mind blows and shifts — till I forgot

if you own God? Name one: so you may say,
he pardons you. I have none. I do not.

VI

Breaking

Alone, I lean to breathe, from my own window
out from the upstairs back room with no child —
over the garden: out to the light rain.
Behind the grey, lopped trees, deep rails glint:
one way, London and the high-lit rooms,
north, the humming towns and there between
roots: the inescapable Midlands.
Trains shake the house; I have been both ways, now
I stare across the grass, snowed dark with leaves
with ragged massive yellow walnut leaves
I should rake up; but cats and fieldmice rustle,
spiders and woodlice hide there. Fine, soft rain
to end eyes' ache — I turn

                    and you are there,
dogged and dark. The room, stripped bare. Sit. Wait.
You smile. And now I know that you are dead:
only the dead smile so, are easy with us
speak truth

                    You cheat me still. I asked you for your life
and now my own swerves back through pain, I know
you told me nothing. Tell me what you love.

'No,' I say soft, 'it is not open, done:
tangled, green as hedges,'

Then, winter's silence.

'Wait:
When you were gardener's boy once, by great houses,
Did you see riding-horses?'

Shut in rows:
Tossing slim heads down bolted doors, as smooth
as polished wood: more kindly fed than children
while their good coats and their soft tempers held.

'So in warm strength, sharp senses, they live close:
these five owned horses I have petted, call,
now by names; as I have known them all,
But sold, the quick names change as light as yours
Byron, boxer —'

                    Eyes withdrawn from anger
glitter — you wave me leave to entertain,
quiet, as the gold horse I show you.
Captain —

yet he will wait. Horses learn patience: you,
strong fingers drumming on the dull, scratched, table
were never — wholly — broken. For your sake
I will give pain a landscape, dredging up
some fragments from my life — clouds; leaves, that sink
outside your room: who always asked too much.
The roots of love pull coldly strange. Again
warmed, rough in my fingers a blue gate
Creaks. I cross the sunlit yard, to Captain.

Though he is not the oldest; though his coat's
still fine, red-gold, he dozes in his stall,
short sandy lashes shut: soft though you coax
only a shoulder twitches, to each call.
Nothing wakes him, stiff as an old general,
the last reserve, the horse which you'd first ride
whose long forelegs still strike out with some grace
but hind legs check — oh rocking horse ! — each stride.

I thought him patient, watched him stoop and still,
while girls bound cloth about each swollen leg;
Until we galloped on the winter hill
of harsh and stony ground; were overtaken
by every horse. Pulled up then, at the rear
he laid his red ears flat, struck from the path
still steamed, sweat-dark, pushed hard to jostle through
To the ride's head: the place he meant to be.

Watch close; is he asleep? Yellow and savage
are teeth his twitched lips bare. His lamed, slim feet
shudder in straw. Though he is gelded, as
stallions to a March cry rear and thrash,
he pounds the gathered dark, out-races age.

This, your weather: autumn's poise,
till frozen leaves shiver
from great ashtrees

when sun at morning meets the eyes
still generous

                when spiders star
miles of silk in cropped grass, lent

a glow which you might call, transparent.

The first,
the last thing
that we are.

Paddy, first owned was barely fed,
his ribs jabbed through
hair dull as mud;
now his brown belly swells
broader than barrels
he grunts while trotting,
crossly, skids
wild across the school —
no warning —

no one's fool
comes hard to learning:

                    Jumps the moon
in pictures shown,
in blue and frost's air
sailing
(though thick-legged as beasts you coaxed
round hedge, dark pondside, ploughing)

from the hay-heaps his rams and cries
scatter rough ponies, reeling:

The horses — twice his weight, and size —
                    From his low nose
Run squealing.

The year of the great dryness:
I saw cracks here two feet deep
dark wounds to set a hand in;
It frightened me, that summer

that it might never rain again
or you
Recover

On paths which horses scramble
mud thick as boots shines blue
cut fresh by their sharp moons of feet.
So you turn, new,

no liturgy for you whose dress
is light —? Earth, rougher than a ring:
weighed down by drought, by heaviness;
you do not answer.

But you sing.

His wall-eye stares, white crystal, blue:
is pure — and cold. Does Patrick think?
High as walls stand; whitening slow
(as greys do, ageing) to instincts
he has added swerves and falls
red jags of pain he would not come to
willingly, once more. So Patrick
I trust most: to come straight home:

Measuring mud, the gate's width: speed:
Jumping, always, as he's asked to:
Doing all things if he trusts you —

Never trust such dignity.
It is Patrick who I see
Die willingly: on hunting ground
　　　Set to high walls; white legs unsound.

Rattling round the low and sunlit bridge
I saw only white ballast, not the rails

as over the abandoned line
we walk, while Sunday sifts and glows, through pale
gravel: thinking idly of the people

who rattled through
while trains still ran

Travelling
I see through time; to us, all dead
quiet as the sunlit earth
at how this land might be:
The same, with all its warmth, all its mistakes —
Or changed — and changed for ever, by a terror
We could not dream:
And worked to make.

There are lists of horses' habits,
weaving, dishing and crib-biting
all are strange, their names exciting,
most are wretched: like wind-sucking —
to breathe in, wrongly, just because it
bores you, breathing. Oscar does it.

Simply stated, it can kill you.
Oscar once must have been bored
near to death, left in a stable.
Now his breath comes gurgling through
swallowed, stifling: who affords
such luxury outside a fable?

Real breath chokes you, held inside —
as he would not be, small horse, racing
even wild Monty down,

warm and strong horse, drumming, breasting
cold wind, thistles. And then, bored;

straps tied round his neck to keep him
out of the familiar hurting
hold him back from solaced eating
silent, fretting,
passion, flawed.

I would tell you at last,
of purest madness
of horses I saw first:
the thoroughbred,
Dancer who came
from desert Arabians,
wild as time —
and hopelessly inbred.

Forget the pride in trappings,
the money, the long names
of owners: straw and cloths
stamped by their feet:
they do not belong by furs and paddocks.
From crooked, blazing light
They rise and leap.

Never would I ride one
the gods must make you mad —
happy to die young.
Monty, the black horse, fires
at sight of open country, whirls through sun
plunges at barbed wire:

was once a show-jumper, once broke a leg:
will kill a man, I think. I watch, and sense —
from Patrick's back — a golden field about him
electrical. He's lost. He is the distance

In the grass fields we meet. He's gentle there.
He has the soft nose of the Arab, slight
dropped to a hand. Only his far eye looks
Past gates and apples, to the speed of light.

Upon slow ground we pass through
      People live:
dark-bricked, beside the railway in rows,
in battered and high flats by the loud road —

while still in mountains, in white silent space
in mist it gleams: the grey unchanging pool.
At one edge, the black pole someone placed:
but no man, ever, lived here. King or fool,
Would its depths return a human face?

Prisoned in a mind, inside a country:
in most oppressive homes:
Like song, like dark that perfect water enters.

How it will freeze our bones.

She rides, I have to tell you, very badly:
against my rhythms: sitting, when I rise.
At intervals I knock her round a gate
To show I'm still resentful, and awake.
In tangled hedges or at tedious cloud
she stares, leaves me in charge: a dangerous rule
she'll learn, with horses from this riding-school.
      The road shines wild with water. The sharp rain
runs along the bridle while I sneeze
and dream of hay-stems tickling down my throat
while plodding the hill-paths through dripping trees.

To the strong rain the sadness disappears
where on the young gold horse in perfect sun
last week I felt the ebbing of the year
white as the dust of gallops, now we come
to the hill's crest, the pure cold of wind.
                       The horses shake
their dozing heads. The mist, the rain-sting take
that tired thought from mind: that seasons doom
and shape us. Shivered harebells bold as eyes
spring blue from whitening grass

                                 here there is room
To gallop, (roughly), dazzled into air
lean only to the horse — spit sour mud
thrown by the rest. Speed sings, throbs, bears
the rising ground's blue rush, till in the wood
the horses steam, tall ivy drips lush green,
Creepers brush our faces

                        I could break
that soft spray — if she'd let me

                            wood still wild
as jungle? Eden? What do you believe?

You. I jerk the horse's head up short.
It is as if a light struck through the trees
but there's no sun. It is a sycamore
yellow and rain-smooth, cloudy, luminous,
it fills me, calmly distant from you, tired
to gentleness: as though you were my friend,
even, my quiet horse. Now I offend.
I brush the glistened neck, the mane's fine nape,
horse, do not knock me round the hillside gate —

I promise nothing, mumbling wet sweet leaf.

no: turning back, across the grey of fields,
I might see many faces. If they met

It is as something free of time, as wild,
Green as the stolen branch. So your warmth spills
on horse's flank, on path, to every place

where they dismount: as cloud becomes the hills.

You will not say — 'I know why you did this'
but tell you, being dead: I once drank down
like you, the white and choking of despair,
from cramp and dazzle rescued, did not drown,
unlike you, had an after; set apart,
learned to make thick pottery; the right
answers to be exiled from a ward
to face the guilty spaces upon forms
to find quite suddenly one quiet night,
a sun-washed morning in a half-cleared room

that nothing, ever, takes the sense of nothing
being possible or right to do
at least by you — hands, on the soft throat, clenched.
Only two reasons come
you did not have before: the faintest sense
that there's an end: a huge and pulsing world
turned lightly, a white air breathed through by rain.
And how they changed, and how uncertain, came
into the strangest cracks of confidence,
those people with bright eyes and fine careers,
who simply said 'I know:' who dared not give
another word. Now, with quick breath held,
you feel along that ledge from which you fell

our longing: where the wave smashed black, to live.

Facing the window, whose red iron rusts,
see horses fade; slow stirring now, they blur

the waves of light. Starred heads shift by a gate;
lifting briefly — not old power;
freedom, a rough offer. Who accepts?

In these closed spaces, tied, they live with men,
brushed and fed and schooled. They are built courses
for races, jumping. Hands which lead them through
barred doors, caress them: dark feet kick them.

Men half-made my horses.

                    Who made you?

You smile, quick audience I scarcely know:
turn again, your skin drawn tight, as now
believing little: sensing much —
black, new space.

                    You stole your closing line.

'Would you have known as much, in life?' I say.

I walked ten miles, buying a first book,
to read my 'poet'; who has taught me, what?
call rough, white water 'silver', be unsure
of raw sight; broken stick, trapped in the stream.
Colours, which glow new-peeled: jays' cries, air blue
tear the wood's mist; still reach me. But before
only the stories: ghosts, and witches: mere
bogies, frightened mind. My sense lay starved.

'Could it think our rooms rich? whose stronger light
might make you flinch; smooth carpet masking floors;
a glowing square where coloured lines might show

anything: new worlds?'

                              as to my tall
grandfather — fire sun-red, he sat late
gazing in those pictures; curled pipe-smoke
tender and incredulous round his chair
he watched skies open — silver, dancing men
drift in the soft moon dust: treading air.

'Don't trust: it shows you other gleaming rooms
all you might own, strange tricks to make you fear,
new bogies. Walk into its room, at night,
and a cold, shut silence fills you there;
the lightless air — Yes: I live so; work
and skim through papers, on the brink of sleep
through bombs and prizes, shiver and forget;
and next day in the slow rain, sleep to work.
So, now, we starve: so richly that we lose
kindness — which is space: enclosed, enclosed.
We make, and buy: but never own a voice.

Yet you spoke? I will tell you: do not flinch,
that your words are not torn, they are still read.
Is there no warmth in this, to comfort you?'

If the warm voice spoke true —
not late, no — but too soon:
How many read? yet write my trust. I still
will speak unspoken pain: what I was then:
The hawk drives down from emptiness to kill.
The land is brutal: you should know how hard.
The thin cats fight for scraps in the grain-yards,
dogs are beaten. Walking, I would see
thin rows of twine stretched tight across a tree,
my stomach caught with sickness; they were hung
with weasels, twisted, dancing, mouldered skin;
with black crows shot to pieces. Men would say
'the keeper does this, to keep pests away;'

129

the killing is inside us. Clear autumn saw — ah, what
would you call it, my season? the trusting sow's throat cut.

Then they gave me allowances, they said
You will have time to write. But not enough.
She worried for the children; then we moved
To Northborough, the fens, damp, low and dark.
I scarcely slept. I could not write at all;
I had no strength to bind again the small
things I have told you of; goldfinches; gleam
of frost in air, as winter dammed all streams.
One night I woke, choked with black breath and fear
and still by Patty's side, ground on the quilt
with empty hands; lest I should cry to her.

Yet she returned. What did I say, before?
You must not think her beautiful.
Her teeth were pointed, her quick mouth too long —
her smile not that perfect outer light
but flaring, deep, inside. I felt, not saw,
her turning to me, in the empty room,
her hand warm round a book I had not read.
From then, I felt, I knew:
though I could not admit: that she was dead.
Only the dead are easy with us, smile
will never cheat

          do you think yet, or guess
that links may come between us, fine as silk
which stretch and bear for ever: cannot break?

'I. . I would believe so,' having found
songs he wrote for Patty, after years
in the asylum: naming her: still kind,
green and secret as the unfenced land.

But she did not come often. I took spades
to that sad ground; and stopped; mocked by the sun

in my eye-corners. I was gone
in days, to silence, over angry fields.

'They certified you mad.'

With reason: as I slopped their thin grey food,
I was, too soon, the earth. I chose too late:
a husk of dark: but throbbing through me rose
cool orchids' mouths, white foam of cuckoo flower.
I slept for seasons. Night's room filled my head;
flashed past the constellations, autumn skies.
Behind the steady Plough, swift Pegasus,
the harvest's homeless stars glowed in my eyes.

Where is she gone? She has laid down my pen —
the living rise too quick! crosses white boards,
traces my name on glass, where her mouth blurs

orchards — mist light as bird:
breath flickers, comes

Wait — I am not Clare:

who once, I loved,
or her, with pale loosed hair. I saw no choice.
Called into closed space I turn, my voice
echoing last light between them both
bent to the sill (strange visit's end) they watch
bullfinches: scattered apples in frost's branches.
He whistles through high glass. They glow, take flight;
the hazed sun, chill rose, in the webs of white

where light is fear. Laid in the low sick room
my torn head aches; so, stubborn, I would sink

in the dark root, the silence, but there's none.
The broken stars rise in us

                         the low fire
mutters, is the wind, is all I hear;
him ill, I cannot write, no, not his name.
I stare through light: soft gold, flames tire
tremble through young twigs. Come —

see, torn love, whose face
turns tender, half-lit fields,
how strong a kindness flares beneath desire:
enclosed as the blind fire
holds heat: here in
                a shuttered room ash quivers
                the hawk, the lark's white sun.

                Sunk from whirled flight, from fear,
                Her hand burns silver: lies.

I wake untouched. My cold lips ache,
I yawn, brush black hair, sing.
Deep in March root wind turns,
dark woods glow. Riding, free,

the broken ground, your dust, breathes;
earth kindles air; love sees.

IV
Turkey

Turkey, 1982

I

As my feet reached the plane door
I felt the old rain touch my face,
I crossed scuffed metal. The steward said
'Good morning —' like a sharp reproach:
For it is day.

            I hold no fear
Of flying. I need only be.
The wing is tilted and the dew
Of cloud blows on it. Then the sun,
A steady line upon the rim.

Below, the Alps — sharp sunlit wall.
My neighbour crowds the light to see.
'Where are you going?' Istanbul.
The unfelt heat, blue minarets
Dance to my eyes, invisibly.

But, white air, I do not say
That we go forward or we change:
I could yet brood, in this still space,
On rivets a machine made stay,
On perfect metal, smeared by hands.
I met a woman once who swam
The coldest water — yet must try
To daze herself with drink to fly.

Where are you going? Istanbul:
Colourless name. All I have found,
Carpets; dust, kisses, I may say,
When my winged feet are back on ground.

They have lost my baggage. It has flown
With the swallows to Izmir. Or somewhere —
They have lost the car, firmly reserved,
'What reservation? Perhaps, tomorrow
I will come to your hotel.'
The Sunday voice has left the phone
Ground burns my feet. The slow bus stalled.

But one man showed us, all the way
The broken walls, the careless gulls,
The horses, still in traffic. I
Understand this city. Why
Should anything work all the time?
At the hotel we do exist,
See, we are down on paper, dim
Kind shabby life. They open wide
Balcony doors from this high room:

Hills with the leap of minarets
The glittered waters of the Horn
My guidebook calls polluted — yet
The slow boats drift askew, they cross.
The rooftops bristle crazy masts
Of aerials. The tiles are new,
The house walls crumble, even as
The tattered carpet in the room
Has every shade of wave and rose.

Old women in white headscarves lean
Across their balconies and stare —
And suddenly the swifts are there
In the sun's rose and dazzling air
With fluttering harsh cries they cross
Sweep cliffs of houses, rise and pass:

Is Africa a wing's space there
The low sun, God? A hooting car

Carries, in wreaths, quick crimson flowers,
Sweeps the street's corner. Life or death
In this new flow, I cannot guess,
Yet understand the voices raised,
Football in alleys, though each word
Is strange to me, and rags of cloth
Flutter from broken balconies.

Not child, or bird, or perfect air
Still I sit, in my one dress
Hear women talk, swifts dip, and press
My toes in the old rug's deep blue:
Till day's wings lose the Bosphorus.

III

Zoe, the road to Adipazari is greasy with rain.
Did you come to the Black Sea for summer, impatient body
Twitching under thin sheets? Empress —
How shall I come near you? What name did the husbands find,
The young man whom you took, at sixty-four:
The third: the last?

               Rain-plastered; chickens stalk
House-sills; calves lie in roadside dips
Black hips hunched to the ground. Is the clay truly you
The high mosaic, the red hair slipping
Over the pearls; the dry, brocaded throat?

Soaked women crouch in trucks, slipping on melon.
In the mosaic, the Virgin's harsh black eyes
Stare straight. But you are smiling, glancing sideways
At her, or at your lover, on the right.
(They ripped the old stones out, for his new face.)
Your smile is sad. Is it, then, harder: being older?
Tell me — No, you say, the people loved me.
(Your voice is rain, quick birds above the cypress
The storm which floods the straggling melon flowers.)

137

I lived past seventy — still straight:
They loved me.

What did you love?

No, your smile
Flickers and fades, into the station's air.
A boy, bent forward in a high peaked saddle
Hustles a smoke-grey pony, rattles stones,
Home, home, the light is over.

The great trains
Shudder in steam: two engines, joined to go
Over the mountain ridge, to Karabuk.
The steam is spilling, foaming. The red light
Out of the fire box, leaps, across its white:
The engines breathe, quick, hoarsely, like the dying
Who will not leave us, who will not let go:
The new face closed as stone. The whistle screams
Fading to softness, as a night bird flying.
Now, as they are gone towards the tunnel,
The brakes beat and the pistons heave: see, Zoe,
The red points turning off into your dark
Small as a ring glints, on a finger, as
The trailed light from the driver's cigarette.

My luggage, lost in Istanbul
Held some illusions. Now, to cling
To childlessness, a monthly wage,
Closes, a cage, a lightless thing:
And though I fear all risks: all harms:
Yet I lie tumbled in those arms.

The rain is over. Will I have a child?
I hear you laughing at me, shake your head,
The fine skin of your cheeks, so oddly soft
Trembles; does not touch me. You had children,
I do not think they mattered much to you,
Clever, desiring. Ask the young man what
You cared for: he would not know everything.

The people know, who seem to stare so straight
As I go yawning in the milder light:
Where sheep wrench grass between the railway tracks
A cat, warmed on iron roofs, teases its tail.
You comb long hair, parting the new white roots;
Pearls glisten skin. The tracks steam last night's rain,
Wet in the sheep's mouth, moist on the melon's rim —
I will not say goodbye. I spring
Off rails to space, glance sideways, once again.

IV

Birnaz and Gönül, in the sun
One in the yard, one on the balcony
Of their shared house, heard children run
Telling of the strange woman in
A white car — So they ask me in.

Birnaz swells, in flowered skirts,
Her eyes consider. Gönül spins
A tight black dress, blows smoke and laughs.
The neighbours' children pile, with me,
In the best room, on pink divans.

The ancient trains you photograph
Clank by; through drifts of steam as white
As Birnaz' curtains. She brings tea,
White flaking cheese, the perfect bread.
'Eat more, *I* made it!' She can speak
No English. I can mutter 'Thank you.'
Gönül writes out rows of names:
Birnaz' two girls, her son's; I clasp
My green beads round small Derya's neck.
Sharp, brown, she chews through sunflower seeds.
Two girls of fourteen, cousins? swing
Pale ankles. Each clear face is cream,

Eyes, not quite black, shine quick, amused.
Families, moons, are not the same,

We change. Now I find photographs:
My taller sister. They would know,
Birnaz' hands say, from the face,
One of the two grandmothers
Snaps green-skinned beans on to a plate.
Am I delaying dinner? But
Nobody frets. They sit; we thumb
Pictures of Birnaz, blurred and young.
Gönül's son drags in plastic guns.
Birnaz and Sereh, the moon's child
Beg photographs, to take and keep:
Our wedding, in that warmed, white room —
'Thank you.' 'Goodbye — ' You are there
By the low window. Birnaz knows
Your name now, runs, to bring you in.

A crescent in the chickens' yard
We swell before the camera; I
Must be there too — they pull me in.
Gönül and the grandmother
Plait arms around me; Derya has
Been pulled, squeaking, through a starched dress.

She howls, as we stand by the car.
Birnaz tugs me. 'You have not
Kissed her.' So, neglectful too
In Turkish, I bend down and rub
Her hair, spiked up by her changed dress,
Kiss her wet face. Yes, she has stopped.
There are more languages to learn.

I have not seen the photographs.
I have the address, in Gönül's quick
Impatient hand. (She kissed me twice.)
I must record that the next day
When you stopped by the rails to take

One last black train, a blue police van
Shot out, to chase us all away.
The Black Sea floats, turned trembling, grey
Ankara floods. I know, again
Chatting; of us too? shelling beans
Birnaz and Gönül watch the rain.

V

We spend five hours in Karabuk:
First, tea: with the Traffic Manager
Whose grey hair waves, a General's.
He is a great man too, he sits
On a wood platform: underneath
The wearied mask of Ataturk.
First he harangues a thin man with
A green wool waistcoat; who withdraws
In bent sad height — being more tall
Than the Great Man. He brings our tea.

Ushered across the greasy track
We sit round the shed foreman's room
Where more tea comes, red-brown in glass.
The hunched grey foreman smokes and sifts
Through phrasebooks, then the printed book
Of Turkish engines. (Ismail claims
His face smiles from one photograph.)

I smile; sit; lapped in the deep sounds
Of steam, its cloud before the cloud
Of steelworks where the mountains part.
The friend we met two days ago
Upon a platform, worries: surely
You are bored? You hunt no trains,
You take no photographs. I swim
In the kind smoke of others' lives,
In haze of tea, the netted charts
Where trains in hundreds cross on lines.

The foreman signs pink forms, as I
Sign forms. Their desks, I understand,
But not the sheds, panting their smoke,
Wild radio music, swirling round.

In their kitchens, by hot, black stoves,
We sit for lunch: of coloured rice
Dark chicken; then the sweet stewed grapes
The nervous foreman will not eat,
But smokes again. More tea, red tea,
Another office: Ataturk
Grown shabbier; small photographs
Wedged under glass on Ismail's desk.

The managers have gone. We see
These photographs. Ismail with gun,
Young in the army then; for whom
Was he shooting? Ismail
With raki raised — the easy laugh.
But all the room is crackling, dark
Men's eyes, fast slogans, 'Lenin, Marx'
Ismail cries. The rest accuse
'Communist!' Then he backs down
The drink-hot, blue eyes wary: 'No — '
The blurred words 'Social Democrat'.
What shall I tell them, now, I am —
Still they take sides. The moist-lipped cook
Counting out tokens, is dismissed
'Fascist!' The black Ataturk
Is jabbed at. All I understand
Is their passion: still they ask
Life to be better. Ismail rides —
He makes wild gestures when he sees
My horse's picture: hands raised in
Impossible speed. The engines wait
Forgotten, warm in rain, in steam.

Day falls apart in formal speech.
We leave the book — I did not think

That they would look so sad. Ismail
Grasps my hand. They pull me in
To stand by them in photographs.
Is that why we came, photographs?

Five hours gone: I quite forget.
We go to shake the Great Man's hand
Decline his tea. The tall man stands
Outside his door, within his call.
We smile: 'Goodbye.' And all his face
Is radiant, the untouched gift.

We leave our friend, the pianist,
Who sat on cliff-tops while we swam
Watching black ants on patient paths.
He takes the bus to Ankara
In headlong rain. For half a day
We miss him, though we drive to sun:

And we miss people, in this car,
The unfelt touching that is care,
Till the hills rise into the haze
Of the Aegean; in my ears
The dry lust of the cicadas.

VI

Bandirma crumbles into sea.
No tourists have come here. And soon
People on balconies crowd, and stare
As though I walked the ghostly moon.

The hotel staircase spirals high
Through warrens of damp, dirty rooms.
Who are the women padding round
The sunlit salon, second floor
With moon-pale faces, heavy eyes?
Singers, from the club next door?

143

But the hotel has been first class —
It says, in English, on signs hung
Beside the Aegean Army's long
First proclamation. 'I would ask
My people now not to enforce
The personnel to use their guns.'

The small mosquitoes bite all night
They whine, they land. What I have done
To sleep in this pink dirty room
I scarcely care. I sleep, they bite,
Bandirma crumbles into sun.

Water, the white pure element
Carries me over, parts and sways.
I watch the quick clear jellyfish
Circle the current, take their way:
Yet know, as the great light sweeps higher,
That we drown sometimes from desire.

VII

I have climbed to the ruins, to beaks of towers
Pointing to sea, their clean white mortar
Shedding thin brick, shedding the glinting quartz.
The field's weeds bring jabbing burs
Into my heels. Yes, the day prickles.
The men are fishing — 'I think you are better
To sun-bathe,' they told me, very politely,
The English teacher, his ambition
Smouldering in the little port,
Hassan, who hated Germany
Yet worked there for five months; who came
To talk to us through the easy light
Where we sat together on yesterday's beach.

Then a night in their small house, the morning yard
Dappled by one tree; the white chicken, dozing

144

Drooped on its plastic sack, in shade.
The children taught me Turkish numbers,
Bir, iki, uç — So now I count
Their hours upon a shadeless beach.
The teacher's wife turns restless, twitching
Ringed hands through brown-gold hair; she comes
From the village; her husband reads; he says
She cooks very well. Yet he once knew
A Norwegian girl — On the bare stone beach
Lifia wanders, twirling her hat
Cuffing her children, quick as a cat;
She swims with a lazy wriggle of shoulders
Under the water, again, again
Tries to pull me under.
                        I will not drown.
I jump back shaking, in blood-warm sea
She shivered at. She cannot make me —
She pulls faces at me for hours. Now I
Climb to the ruins.

This is not my country
Leaves Lifia sad and wasteful, wild
As the dusty field, where few sunflowers grow,
Their yellow flame burnt out to black
They crackle seed —
                        I have grown ill
With sun. I doze in Lifia's room,
On the delicate blue of her striped divan,
Under the fringed white of her sheets.
She mimes and lights
She says I am pregnant,
Arches her stomach. Into the night
We walk to the village party. 'There'
Her husband said, 'the women dance.'

Lean back from hips, step forward, pause:
Shuffle, sway. The yard is lit
By one bulb which a clothes peg clips
To the washing line. The mothers sit,

The young girls dance on modest heels
In ruffled skirts, new-washed, fluffed hair.
Their water is switched off by night; such drought
Cracks the ground. The younger boys
Crouch on a bench. Down-yard, the men
Bright-eyed outside the light's ring, sit
On concrete blocks, smoke, cough and stare —
Arms on each other's shoulders — where the girls
Move on: untouchable.

Daughter: son: be your own country
Come out of this waste: this keeping apart.
The teacher stubbed his cigarette
Stared through lace curtains, greying light.
'The rich get richer, while the poor
Grow poorer.' The baked furrows lie,
Rustle white stalks, in the dried-up yard.

Eyes cracked with salt, head swimming sun
I lie in a dead branch's shade
Until Urzlam, the youngest girl
Comes to me, biting sunflower seed
Two boys have brought to Lifia:
She breaks apart the burnt-out sun,
She crackles, sighs: light-breathed, she sleeps.
There is a city in my eyes
I found along the high field, tiles,
Smashed painted pots. Pick pieces, make
Once more: a place that never was:
In the high air of flying, in
The arching hands, in Lifia's smile.
In the cathedral, the roof glitters,
Live as the scales, the fish he killed.
Pigeons beat above a pillar
Nest unharmed. I look, I learn
All Istanbul's postcards say wrong:
The woman with the cold red hair
Is not Zoe: who has great eyes,
A pointed chin; I think she crushed

Honey for breakfast from frail combs,
Like Lifia: dark, kinder, sure.

My son, my daughter, as I lay
On that bare shore, I heard the day
Spin beneath me, the old world
Spring warm, returning engines hum:
Barefoot, we touch through sun's burnt clay
Gold scrawled with black: Byzantium.